A Journey of Love

A Journey of Love

The Special Children Who Inspired Me to Find and Follow My Passion

Hazel Allen, RN

Order this book online at www.trafford.com
or email orders@trafford.com

Most Trafford titles are also available at major online book retailers.

Printed in Victoria, BC, Canada.

ISBN: 978-1-4269-0595-7

*Our mission is to efficiently provide the world's finest, most comprehensive book publishing
service, enabling every author to experience success. To find out how to publish your book, your
way, and have it available worldwide, visit us online at www.trafford.com*

Trafford rev. 11/2/2009

 www.trafford.com

North America & international
toll-free: 1 888 232 4444 (USA & Canada)
phone: 250 383 6864 ♦ fax: 812 355 4082

This is my story, inspired by one incredible disabled girl and by the children before and after her who have taught me that every life is a treasure to be cherished forever.

This journal is dedicated to my family and to those children and their families with whom we are fortunate to share life.

To Mo, my husband, my best friend, Dad to our two sons, Grandpa to our four grandchildren and partner in every sense of the word to our "special kids." I could not have fulfilled the life I have without his love and understanding.

To our son Glen, another pillar in my life who, like his Dad, has been so involved in his brother's life and in the lives of our "special kids." He is now a husband and an amazing father to Jonathan and Kelsey. Thank you for being you, Glen.

To Greg, our second born, who is the reason I have been able to understand my purpose for being here, my "calling" in life. For this, Greg, I am forever grateful — thank you! He is an incredible father to Veronika and Karolina.

To my extraordinary editors, a huge thank you, not only for your inspiration to complete this project but for your faith that I could actually do it!

Edie Clifton, my long-time friend and colleague. You were the first to tell me that this venture was worth completing and the first to edit a very basic draft.

Glen, our son, who gave not only the time and expertise but endless advice and encouragement to see me through all phases from the incomplete journal to this, the finished product.

Vincent Vachon, a friend of Glen's, who arrived in my life just in time to add the finishing touches to edit and submit for publishing *A Journey of Love*.

And to my brother, Dan, thanks for the pen to sign my journal!

I know for sure that every person in the world has a purpose for being here — a calling. The work of your life is to discover that purpose and get on with the business of living it out. The only courage you need is the courage to find and follow your passion.

Oprah Winfrey, September 2003

INTRODUCTION

"Welcome to Holland"

I am often asked to describe the experience of raising a child with a disability — to try to help people who have not shared that unique experience to understand it, to imagine how it would feel. It's like this...

When you're going to have a baby, it's like planning a fabulous vacation trip — to Italy. You buy a bunch of guide books and make your wonderful plans. The Coliseum. The Michelangelo David. The gondolas in Venice. You may learn some handy phrases in Italian. It's all very exciting.

After months of eager anticipation, the day finally arrives. You pack your bags and off you go. Several hours later, the plane lands. The stewardess comes in and says, "Welcome to Holland."

"Holland?!?" you say. "What do you mean Holland?? I signed up for Italy! I'm supposed to be in Italy. All my life I've dreamed of going to Italy."

But there's been a change in the flight plan. They've landed in Holland and there you must stay.

The important thing is that they haven't taken you to a horrible, disgusting, filthy place, full of pestilence, famine and disease. It's just a different place.

So you must go out and buy new guide books. And you must learn a whole new language. And you will meet a whole new group of people you would never have met.

It's just a different place. It's slower-paced than Italy, less flashy than Italy. But after you've been there for a while and you catch your breath, you look around...and you begin to notice that Holland has windmills...and Holland has tulips. Holland even has Rembrandts.

But everyone you know is busy coming and going from Italy...and they're all bragging about what a wonderful time they had there. And for the rest of your life, you will say "Yes, that's where I was supposed to go. That's what I had planned."

And the pain of that will never, ever, ever, ever go away...because the loss of that dream is a very very significant loss.

But...if you spend your life mourning the fact that you didn't get to Italy, you may never be free to enjoy the very special, the very lovely things...about Holland.

Emily Perl Kingsley, 1987

For reasons that I will share with you as my story evolves, I am a registered nurse. I was, and perhaps still am, a paediatric nurse. I am the second eldest of a family of seven raised in a small village on Vancouver Island.

I wanted, and needed, to share this story. Our precious foster child Jenelle is the inspiration. It has taken me some time to realize how my passion in life — to be able to care for her — happened. I did not plan on going to Holland, but the journey there was incredible...

GEORGE

My journey started a great many years ago with my eldest brother George, who is two years older than me. At that time we lived in Qualicum Beach, a small village on central Vancouver Island. Our Mom tells us that in 1943, when George was five years old, he often came in from play and would want to "have a rest 'cause my leg hurts." Our parents soon noticed that whenever he was playing, his right leg would swing out and he often couldn't run in a straight line. Apparently he had fallen out of a tree and they felt that was probably the reason. When they took him to the local physician, Dr. East, he agreed. The problem didn't improve.

Dr. East made arrangements for George to be seen by a specialist, Dr. Simpson, some one hundred miles south in Victoria. As we didn't have a car, Mom and George made the trek by bus.

* * *

In August of 1944 our family moved south from Qualicum Beach to another small village, Shawnigan Lake.

On October 31st of that year, Mom again took George to see Dr. Simpson in Victoria. He told Mom that George had to go to the Queen Alexandra Solarium, a hospital for crippled children at Mill Bay, about five miles from Shawnigan Lake. George stayed there from November of 1944 until November 1945. He was diagnosed with *Legge Calve Perthes Disease*.

* * *

Mom's recollection (Dad passed away in 1991) of the information they were given at that time is remarkable when compared to the information given today. In a medical journal today it does agree with 1944 in terms of the signs and symptoms: "There is pain in the thigh and groin, it may go down the front of the thigh to the knee. Movement of the hip may be restricted and painful." The treatment today, however, differs totally!

* * *

During the year George spent in the Solarium, he became quite notorious. He was not to put any weight on his right leg. Not surprisingly, at five years of age he was unaware of the consequences of "misbehaving." In order to ensure that he followed the protocol for treatment, he was put into a full body cast. Before his year had ended, however, he had learned how to slip out of the cast and acquire some freedom!

Mom tells me that often at the beginning she had to try to hide her tears as it came time for visiting hour to end. If George saw her tears he would say, "if you don't cry, Mom, I promise I will get better faster."

* * *

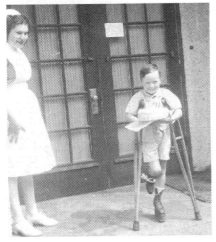

One of his favourite nurses during this time was Edith. We would always be able to remember her as in June of 1945, some seven months after George had been admitted we had a new sister; her name is Edith.

Five days after Edith was born, George celebrated his sixth birthday. I was never permitted to visit George for fear of bringing childhood germs into the hospital. His birthday was celebrated with his friends who were also spending a part of their young lives in the Solarium.

As far as my memory goes back, I have known I wanted to be a nurse, a nurse who would help kids like my brother. I would imagine this time in my life was what ultimately influenced my career choice.

* * *

In September of that year, George started grade one as an inpatient student. By November, my understanding is the staff was getting somewhat perplexed by the amazing ability of this young man to maneuver his way into weight bearing on his affected leg. Mom and Dad thought they could manage him better at home and so, reluctantly, the doctor agreed to let them try. It was a good decision; parents' eyes were everywhere, then as now!

It was wonderful for all of us to be together for the first time in a year. George was now able to walk on crutches. Over the next two years, he learned to go from a stroll to a sprint to a race winner on those two sticks. His right leg was fastened in a harness so that he was unable to touch the ground, in this way his hip continued to heal. His left shoe had a three-inch lift, so that if he were to stand without the harness his right foot remained off the ground. At bedtime I could help him into his brace which kept his leg straight through the night. It looked uncomfortable but he never complained; it was the way it had to be. Over the years I was to learn that, with kids, treatments that just "had to be" were accepted much more easily by the child than by their loved ones.

* * *

During his convalescence, George taught us that being on crutches for years had some interesting challenges. Our school was some two miles from home and there were no school buses. It was too far for George to walk. In good weather our neighbour, Jacky, three years older than

George, gave him a ride on the crossbar of his bicycle. The crutches balanced on the front handlebars. To my knowledge there was never an accident with this mode of transportation.

In inclement weather, if Dad were available he gave both George and I a lift to school. Some days I wished for rain or snow when Dad was working as then Constable Ross, the local RCMP officer, would arrive in the police car to transport us. I was always proud of my brother, and still am, but on those days I felt like a princess as we passed all our friends walking in the rain!

George did become very fast on his crutches and could actually win foot races with his peers. He was able to throw his crutches very wide and take extended strides. The village store was very close to our home and often George was asked to go for groceries. He would have a bag in each hand and still be able to manipulate his crutches to get everything home safely. Apparently Mom was often criticized for making him do such things. Those thoughts were, I'm sure, instilled in my mind to be used years later.

Some three plus years since he had been able to stand on his right leg, George was told he would be able to walk. It was not easy. The doctor had told our parents he could walk from the living room to his bed. It took several attempts over time to be able to accomplish this feat.

Eventually, George did fully recover. He became very active in sports both as a child and continues as an adult.

He is a retired professional engineer, married and the father of four. Two of his sons, Sean and Mike, will have chapters of their own.

SEAN

The second influential individual I encountered on my "life journey" was George's first born son Sean. Sean was born in 1962, the first grandchild on our side of the family. He was healthy, adorable and weighed in at 8 pounds 3 ounces.

I had started my three-year registered nurses training at the Royal Jubilee Hospital in Victoria, BC, in 1960. George and his wife Sylvia, and now Sean, were living in a small logging camp some forty miles away.

Very shortly after he was born, Sean developed a red scaly patch on the back of his head. By three months of age Sean would experience severe skin reactions that were of concern more to his parents than to the medical professionals. His diaper area was constantly raw. Soon all of his body orifices would be reddened, scaly and very uncomfortable. Gradually his parents would notice that Sean's pressure points, his elbows, his buttock, his knees, his heels and always the back of his head were affected.

Sean would be in and out of hospital for the next several months. Many doctors saw him but no one could give George and Sylvia the answers they sought.

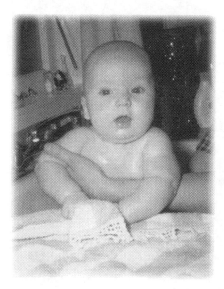

Eventually, he was unable to retain his food and had relentless diarrhoea.

One of the queries his parents had was that they thought the skin problem seemed to have intensified when Sylvia had weaned him from breast milk. Still the doctors were unable to come up with a diagnosis.

During his hospitalizations I would be able to spend time with him as I lived in the nurses residence adjoining the hospital.

Sean's condition continued to deteriorate and he died in June of 1963 at eleven months of age.

Shortly after his death, his parents were informed by their doctor that Sean's disease had been identified. He had *acrodermititis enteropathica*, a genetic disorder that appears in the first few months of life or after cessation of breast-feeding. This disease affects the skin and the digestive tract. There was no known cure. They were told that chances of having another child with the disease were rare.

TOMMY

Mo and I were married in 1964 and moved to Nanaimo, BC. Mo was stationed there with the Royal Canadian Mounted Police. I had applied to work on Paediatrics at the local hospital. I started my employment on the maternity ward, as there was no position available on Paediatrics. The schedule rotated us between the delivery room, the nursery and the ward.

In November I was working in the delivery room when a young Mom gave birth to a baby who had obvious physical deformities. In those years there were not often tests available to forewarn doctors or parents of the possibility of complications. Frequently, parents were advised to leave the baby, go home and try to get on with their life without the child. Before she left the hospital, the Mom named her son Tommy.

My next rotation sent me to the Nursery where the Nurses cared for Tommy. If we were busy, he was fed, burped and settled; if we were quiet, he would be fed, burped, cuddled and then cuddled some more. Some of us would stay late or pop in on our time off to make sure Tommy had an extra cuddle. He was on a waiting list to be transferred to Woodlands, an institution in Vancouver for handicapped children who needed a home.

Just before Christmas that year there was an opening on Paediatrics and the day I started on the ward, Tommy was transferred there. He was too old for the newborn nursery and was still on the wait list for a transfer.

It was my pleasure and privilege to introduce and teach the staff all I knew about Tommy. Once again he was the centre of our world when we had a lull on the ward. When we were busy it often broke my heart when we had to ignore his "fussy" cry with more emergent cases.

The candy stripers, young girls who volunteered after school and on weekends, were his gift as they could spend uninterrupted time with Tommy.

It was with mixed emotions that we said our goodbyes to Tommy when the call came for him to be transferred to Woodlands. We drew straws to see who would make the trek to Vancouver with him. It was difficult to believe; I was blessed by being chosen to accompany him to his new home.

For some months we would be in contact to see how he was adjusting to his new surroundings. Those communications became less frequent.

I did visit him once when we were in Vancouver. He seemed happy. His demands were limited. Perhaps his physical and mental limitations made life easier for him, but it didn't make it easier for me to leave him!

Over the years I would occasionally think of Tommy, I still do! We were transferred to Ottawa in 1967. I was pregnant and our life was busy. I would never know where Tommy's life would take him.

GLEN

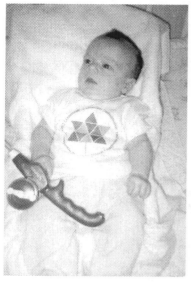

Our son Glen was born in June of 1967 in Ottawa. For several months before he was born, I would talk to myself about the probability that our baby would have some form of disability. It would be OK. We could deal with it.

When Glen arrived, it was with hesitation that I accepted our young son as a perfect, healthy, happy baby. The thoughts I had quickly disappeared and we became a very content family of three.

* * *

Our family dynamics changed in the years to follow. Glen's personality, I believe, was shaped a great deal by those family dynamics. He is a very quiet, sincere, empathetic young man.

* * *

Over the years, Glen has continued to be a wonderful, caring son. He and Leona were married in 1997. Jonathan arrived in 2001 and Kelsey followed in 2005. Someone once told me that you will know what kind of parent you have been when you see what kind of parent your child becomes — I think we did a good job!

Glen has done well. He has a degree in English Literature from the University of Victoria and went on to obtain a Masters Degree in Business Administration doing one semester in Hong Kong and another in Malaysia.

He spent time teaching in Hokkaido, Japan. He was Manager of the International Centre for Students at the University of Lethbridge in Alberta for two years. Glen and Leona returned to Victoria in 2006, where he is now a faculty member at Camosun College.

Glen will be an integral part of the chapters that follow.

GREG

Our second son arrived in May of 1969 in Ottawa. Unlike my first pregnancy, I never thought of having a child with health concerns. The only question was whether Glen would have a brother or sister.

On May 2nd our question was answered and Glen had a brother, but there was a "problem." Our doctor, Dr. Nuyens, decided to administer a touch of gas to put me to sleep for a few minutes.

When I woke, the fact that our baby had been taken from the delivery room did not frighten me. From my few months working in the delivery room, however, it should have set off alarms.

The nurse eventually told me that we had a son. I had actually planned on a daughter, Colleen, but a Gregory was even better; we had lots of baby boy clothes!

Dr. Nuyens then appeared and told me that not only did we have a son but that our son had been born with deformed arms. I still remember my concern for Mo and how he would react when we told him. My concern was quickly answered as Dr. Nuyens had already spoken with Mo. His biggest concern was how *I* would respond when I was told.

When I was taken from the delivery room to the ward I would appreciate the amazing qualities of my husband: he had met Greg, he had accepted Greg, he had acknowledged that we had been given a challenge with which we could cope.

It was several hours before I was introduced to our son. His disability was more severe than I had imagined. The following days passed as a dream. I would imagine waking from this dream to be at home and still pregnant. The news we had been given was just a dream. I didn't want to wake up in case the dream was a reality.

* * *

The many doctors who examined Greg wanted us to know that we could leave him in the hospital for a short time or place him in care forever. Not for a moment did we consider either possibility. We had our second son and he had a brother at home waiting for us; we were now a family of four.

* * *

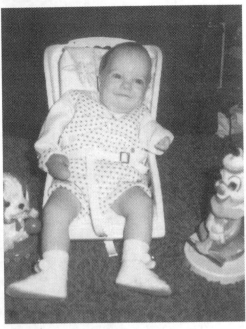

My Mom had made the trek from Vancouver Island to Ottawa to be with Glen while I was in hospital. It had been an adventure for her as Air Canada was on strike. Dad had driven her to Seattle and her flight had taken her from there to JFK Airport in New York. From there she had taken a train to Montreal. Canada had a challenge of its own at the time; history would refer to it as the FLQ crisis. In the days that followed Greg's arrival, we were so thankful that Mom had braved the circumstances of flying through unknown territory. She would make the initial phone calls to family to tell them of Greg's arrival.

We had incredible neighbours and friends in Ottawa who were there to welcome our son as just another baby in the circle of life. There were lots of hugs and lots of tears from lots of people in those first few weeks.

Mom had planned on staying for a few weeks. One evening she announced that she would be leaving sooner; she realized that not until we were alone would we be able to acknowledge fully the dramatic turn our lives had taken.

* * *

Medically, Greg was diagnosed as *bilateral phocomelia*, a congenital disorder that presents as very short or absent long bones. In layman's terms, it is an amputation of the upper extremities. It was most frequently connected with pre-natal exposure to the anti-nausea drug Thalidomide, although I had not taken the drug. There were mixed messages as to what his care should be. There was concern that internal organs might be affected. Our son endured more exams and diagnostic tests in those first few weeks of his life than many of us will endure in our entire lifetime!

All reports returned negative for any adverse involvement of his internal organs. We soon knew his legs were very strong, that his appetite was great and that his heart-warming responses dispelled any concerns about his mental state. He was a content, happy, healthy baby.

* * *

My coping mechanism at the beginning was to keep Greg bundled so that others could not share his deformity. He was my baby and it took time for Mo and Glen to assure me that others would accept and love Greg as we did. Time would show it was easier for some than for others.

* * *

Our first advice for treatment was to take Greg to the Shriners Hospital in Montreal for assessment. When we arrived we were informed that the assessment meant leaving Greg in their hospital for some weeks to be seen by various specialists. We signed the forms and left him to return home to Ottawa. The FLQ crisis was very evident in Montreal with the presence of tanks and military personnel on all the streets.

For any number of reasons, I can remember crying from Montreal until we were very close to home when Glen remarked that he wanted to go see Greg. We turned around, made our way back to the Shriners Hospital and came back to Ottawa with our family of four intact.

* * *

Our paediatrician in Ottawa gave us common sense advice: We were to leave Greg in sleeveless shirts so he could fully mobilize his arms and develop whatever muscles he had. We were encouraged to leave our sons with our teenage babysitter. She had cared for Glen for two years when we had social commitments. He loved her. Greg was a healthy, normal baby and he, too, would love her. She became one of my first links to confirm life could continue as before. There would just be a few more bumpy curves.

* * *

Our next adventure was being referred to the Ontario Crippled Children's Centre in Toronto. There we met a wonderful team. Although the members of the team would change in the ensuing years, they were always willing to listen to us. But, more importantly, to listen to Greg.

The Centre differed from the Shriners Hospital in Montreal in that there was accommodation on site, like a motel, for families. Greg was never admitted to the hospital in all the years he attended; we would all stay together in the rooms provided and he would be seen as an outpatient, even though on occasion he had appointments every day of the week!

* * *

On one of our early appointments it was discussed whether Greg would start with one or two artificial arms. His right side is affected from the shoulder. His left side is about elbow length but malformed. Each arm has a single digit. It was thought, because he had acute sensation in his arms, that to leave the left one without an appliance would be beneficial to him. When he was old enough to make these decisions for himself, he would decide to have only a right artificial arm. He had a left arm that would do most everything he deemed necessary!

* * *

On one of those visits to Toronto, Greg and I went on our own. In between therapy sessions for his prosthetic (artificial) arm, Greg napped on my lap while the older patients staged a talent show.

Earlier that day we had met a girl of eighteen who had recently lost both legs in a tragic car accident. She was having great difficulty learning to walk on her prosthetic legs.

She was the last performer in the talent show. I will never forget the song she sang and the effect that song had on me, even today. It had been made popular by Janice Joplin and is called "Me and Bobby McGee." In one verse she sings "I'd trade all 'o my tomorrows for one single yesterday." That girl in Toronto and the lyrics made any problems I thought we had much smaller; I shed more tears after her singing than I had since Greg was born. The staff was concerned that something had happened with Greg. I assured them that everything was right with Greg. Circumstances for our family were so much easier than for that young lady and her family!

* * *

Those early days were busy. I tend to become over protective with my family so it was a real learning curve for me to share both the boys. After much discussion, I agreed with Mo that it would be good for me if I did a few casual shifts at the hospital. When Greg was eighteen months and Glen three-and-a-half years, I started doing occasional evening or weekend shifts. I loved being back to the nursing challenges and Mo loved having the total care of both boys. The boys loved being with their Dad and having all guy time. Our family was unfolding the way it should.

There were challenges that other families perhaps did not have. We learned to take them in stride and learn from them. We never imagined at the time how we would be able to teach and help other families in the years to follow. It was at this crossroads that I started my involvement in being the best advocate I could be for children with disabilities.

* * *

Living in an area of Canada where winter was severe, dressing Greg for outside play posed some challenges. He needed snowsuits and jackets with one full sleeve for his prosthetic arm and one very short sleeve. My sewing ability was fine for shirts and sweaters but not for heavy outer wear. One day I was buying new snowsuits for both boys at Eaton's Department Store and I asked if they would recommend a tailor who would basically remove an arm from the suit. She questioned why I would want to do that! Several minutes later I was speaking with the Supervisor of the department and the tailor who would not only do it for us but would do it at no charge. For the next several years we would purchase Greg's heavy clothing from Eaton's and the sleeve would be altered with the same acceptance as having trousers shortened!

* * *

Greg started preschool in Ottawa with the group that had been Glen's teachers. We knew them and they knew our family. It was interesting to watch the new kids respond to Greg. It was usually only hours till they were all playing together and automatically helping when help was needed.

Greg became involved with a swim program for kids with disabilities. He and Mo would go off each Saturday morning to join other kids in the pool. Occasionally Glen and I would go along as cheerleaders. It was a very motley but very happy group of kids and volunteers. Mo would be very involved helping some of the boys who would arrive by "bunny bus" without parents. The boys needed help to change into their swimming trunks. He was not a Dad who participated in the pool!

One Saturday, a close friend of ours, Frank Parker, joined Mo and Greg. Frank was a gentle giant at six feet, two hundred and twenty pounds. Greg and Glen loved him. Soon all the kids in Greg's swimming class would love him. Frank went once to see Greg in the pool and ended up going most Saturdays in the years to come. He loved to swim, he loved kids and kids loved him. It was a perfect combination for happiness.

One day Frank came over to talk to me. He was not often serious but this day was different. He shared his thoughts about the bond that he saw between Greg and me. From his observations he believed Greg could be more independent than I was allowing him to be. He was able to think into Greg's years far beyond where we had gone. Frank's children were older than ours were and he could foresee teenage years where having a possessive mother would not be an asset! He said that Greg would be the kind of man that we were moulding now. I promised both Frank and Mo that I would try. (Some days it was easier to keep that promise than others!)

Frank died of cancer in 1991. At his memorial service, I shared the influence he had on our lives. He is a big part of the independent man Greg is today.

* * *

Delving into my box of memories for this period, I uncovered letters from the federal government. They are annoying, even today. We had healthcare coverage with the RCMP, which is a branch of the federal government. They had covered a portion of Greg's first prostheses when he was six months old. As he grew, Greg needed to have ever more involved artificial arms and we had assumed the medical coverage would remain. We were wrong. Replacement and repair costs were not covered. Greg's first mechanical arm in 1972 was ten thousand dollars! In these letters from two different Ministers of Health and Welfare and from the Minister of Finance, one statement reads "it is unlikely that the Allens would be considered persons in need and therefore they would not be eligible for assistance."

We would have to make some lifestyle changes. More letters were written and these ones found in my memory box are a pleasure to reread. From the Shriners organization came word that Greg's prosthetic costs would be covered. In their correspondence there is an apology for the "inconvenience and misunderstanding" that had occurred when Greg had been admitted to the hospital in Montreal. Now he would continue to have the expertise of the Ontario Crippled Children's Centre and be funded by the Shriners organization. This coverage extended from 1972 until 1982 by the Rameses Temple in Toronto and the Khartum Temple in Winnipeg.

As an aside, there is a comment in the letter from John Turner, Minister of Finance and dated May 9th, 1973. It reads "I have also asked the Public Service Group Surgical Medical Plan whether some amendment could be considered to its coverage to provide for artificial limbs and necessary repairs." This policy did come into effect, years later. I would like to think that we had a part in making the difference for other families on their journey with artificial limbs.

* * *

As all families have experiences to look back on years later, ours is no exception. One winter's day when Greg was three we had gone

tobogganing on a small hill near our home. Glen and Greg were on the toboggan and I was sliding along side. The toboggan flipped and the boys fell off, laughing and obviously having a lot of fun. Nearby parents and children, however, were very concerned as Greg's prosthetic arm had done a 180-degree turn! It did look extremely serious! Of course there was no pain and a quick rotation had the arm in the natural position. It was the last time he went to the toboggan hill or the ski hill with his prostheses on! We all learned lessons to remember and to pass on to others in a similar situation.

* * *

As a family we were realizing that Greg and I were making more trips to Toronto to the Crippled Children's Hospital without Mo and Glen. Mo had limited vacation time and it was less expensive if they remained behind. I had incredible guilt leaving Glen so often. Our paediatrician assured us it was the quality of the time I would spend with Glen that would far outweigh the quantity of time. He seemed happy spending days with good friends and nights with his Dad when Greg and I were gone. It was probably more a fact that Greg and I did not want to leave them behind.

We started making inquiries for a transfer where services would be available to Greg. Unfortunately, we thought at the time, there was nothing available in BC. There was in Winnipeg. If we were to move it would have to be Winnipeg or Toronto. Mo's personnel officer strongly recommended Winnipeg if the hospitals were equal. He thought for the type of policing Mo would like to do and for a growing family it would be his preferred choice for us. We were satisfied that the Shriners Hospital in Winnipeg would be acceptable. We would certainly miss the team in Toronto but they had taught us well. I was very happy. We would also be a little bit closer to both our families on Vancouver Island. In July of 1973 we moved from Ottawa to Winnipeg. We would start the next chapter in our lives. It felt right. We were pleased.

* * *

The Shriners Hospital in Winnipeg was a heritage building and as much as it was old it was a delightful place to spend a day. The new team was very accommodating. We all thought it would be a harmonious combination. It wasn't always easy to combine son, parents, physiotherapists, occupational therapists, prosthetists and doctors! We were pleased that once again, as in Toronto, we had a group that would give Greg the best care possible.

* * *

Although Greg was only attending his second year of preschool in Winnipeg, he had already become a teacher. It was not difficult for him to explain that what others saw in his physical appearance was just the way he arrived on earth! He soon had his new friends and teachers completely understanding the way his artificial arm worked and they knew that he would tell them when he needed assistance. We all learned very early not to offer help; he would tell us if help were needed. He is the same today.

* * *

We would soon appreciate the wonderful neighbours we had. Many are still close friends. Most had children of similar ages to Glen and Greg and they as well have remained friends over the years.

* * *

In 1974 we registered Greg for kindergarten at the school where Glen had completed grade one. It was just a block from our house. It was a great shock when we received a letter from the school district office informing us that their understanding was that Greg was disabled and therefore unable to attend the elementary school. Rather, he would be bussed to the school for physically and mentally handicapped children.

After many letters and heated discussions the school agreed to give Greg a trial period from September until Christmas. Needless to say Greg did very well, again teaching both kids and teachers. It was a morning in December I would not soon forget when we met with the school board and the principal from the school. I could not imagine how I would react if the decision were negative. Mo was the calming influence once again. We were quickly assured that Greg would not only continue in the school but that other children in the area would be reassessed to see if they might also be able to attend with their siblings and friends and not be segregated because of a disability.

* * *

There are so many amazing and interesting stories to tell of those first few years as a student! One day I had a call from the school to ask if I would be able to come to help settle a young girl as they were unable to contact her parents. They did emphasize that it was not an emergency but they needed my expertise. Not knowing exactly what that meant I went quickly. It was recess. Greg was playing soccer on the playing field. As he was running down the field his hand had fallen off his artificial arm. He had no feeling of course so he had no idea it had come off. Even if he had, the soccer game was much more important! A new girl to the school, who did not know Greg, had seen what happened and was quite hysterical. Once I identified myself as Greg's Mom and informed her that he was OK, she became interested in what had happened. We often explained that his arm was more like a doll arm and that he didn't hurt when it broke. Simple answers were usually the best; very seldom do children want anything more than simple answers.

* * *

Greg was a member of the Cub Scouts of Canada. One year the boys and their leaders attended a winter survival camp for four days. It was cold! We went for a family afternoon visit and could hardly believe what these boys were enduring and enjoying. We thought Greg would most probably want to return home with us. He definitely wanted to

stay. Apparently the last night was to be the most fun and there was no way he wanted to miss fun! His leaders and friends were pleased he was staying.

* * *

Some time in those years I had been approached by the nursing program at the Grace Hospital about bringing Greg to a class. I had been told so often when Greg was born and in the years following that it was so fortunate I was a nurse, but I was never quite sure why! I had shared these thoughts when I spoke with medical colleagues. I have kept the letter that Greg received from the nursing students thanking him for his willingness to share. It made me feel good that one day, perhaps, one of those students would be able to tell a family in similar circumstances of this amazing young man they had met and how well he was doing. I was very proud of the presentation my son had made.

* * *

Those school years in Winnipeg have so many memories. Some we were privy to at the time and some we learned years later when stories were told from our two adult sons! When Greg had problems connected to his artificial arm he would go from his classroom to the office. The secretary would then call for Glen to come to the office to assist him. Apparently, on occasion, there would be a prearranged time for this to take place. Greg would cause the problem to happen either to escape his class or to help Glen escape his!

Winnipeg winters were often brutal. The boys would leave home for school with snowsuits, mitts, scarves, boots and toques. If Greg should slip and fall he often could not get up. He had, and still does have, incredible abdominal muscles; with winter clothing and icy or snow conditions, however, it was impossible to right himself. Often a friend would see him fall and quickly pull him up. I would occasionally witness this and marvel both at my son and at how he automatically taught others to help.

* * *

Although Greg still enjoyed swimming, he was ready to attempt other sports. Early in his career Mo had been on the Musical Ride, the RCMP's equestrian troupe, and he knew that Greg could ride horses if he chose. We became involved with the Manitoba Riding for the Disabled. Greg was a natural at riding. He soon won ribbons at several dressage competitions.

His next request was to try skiing. Coming from BC we questioned if that were possible in Winnipeg! We soon found that the riverbanks were an ideal slope for all of us to learn. Greg was the only one that became an accomplished skier. He went on to win several gold medals at National and International Disabled Ski Competitions, even becoming a ski instructor on Grouse Mountain in Vancouver at one point.

Greg played soccer in those early years, too. He continued to play into his adult life and, although he may occasionally play for recreation today, I know that he is an avid follower of European "football."

Both boys have not only a love of but also a talent for music. Mo had become interested in the chanter as a precursor to playing the bagpipes, but did not practice and never really learned to play. He had left the chanter out where his sons could see it and soon Glen was fingering tunes and asking questions about taking lessons. We learned that there was a boys' pipe band in Winnipeg. With further inquiries it was discovered that the Lord Selkirk Boy Scout Pipe Band practiced every Saturday morning in our area. Glen joined as a piper and Greg followed soon after as a

drummer. His tenor drum had to be adjusted so that he was able to drum and march. In 1980 Lord and Lady Selkirk invited the band to Scotland. The boys' Pipe Major, Bob Fraser, was from Scotland. He and his wife arranged an extended tour for the band. In 1981 we all went to Scotland. It was an unforgettable experience. When we returned to Canada Glen pursued his interest in the bagpipes and is an accomplished piper today. Greg pursued his interest in playing musical instruments but the pipe and drum band was abandoned.

* * *

For Christmas of 1979 we flew from Winnipeg to spend the season with family on Vancouver Island. It was wonderful to be with family at this special time of the year but we all marvelled at the difference in weather. Christmas Day was sunny and dry and the grass was green. We arrived back in Winnipeg on New Years Day. It was forty below zero, there was a lot of snow, and the wind was harsh.

* * *

Over the next few months we often spoke of the possibility of an early retirement from the RCMP to return "home" to Vancouver Island. The most crucial component would be the options for Greg and his ongoing prosthetic challenges. After a few inquiries we felt confident that this concern could be dealt with.

In September of that year, Glen would be entering grade eight and Greg grade six. If we were going to make the move it seemed the right time in their lives to proceed.

Mo had been doing some picture framing in our basement as a hobby and was thoroughly enjoying it. We decided that perhaps if we had the right location we could start a picture framing business. So, in July of 1980, we left Winnipeg after seven superb years and headed west to Nanaimo. Mo left his career in the RCMP after 25 years. We were excited and hopeful the future would prove we had made the right decision! We did make a pact that we would never say that we should have done things differently — there was no going back.

* * *

In autumn, 1980, Glen enrolled in grade eight at Wellington Junior Secondary School and Greg started grade six at Rock City Elementary. We opened Dogwood Picture Framing Gallery with all four of us contributing to the business, Mo being the Master Picture Framer.

Greg adjusted amazingly well to a new community of friends in the neighbourhood and at school. He became a member of the student council in his first year and the president of the student council the following year. He was very active in the music program and a drummer in the school band. His lifetime love of chess started in those elementary school years.

* * *

Late in 1982 we learned that Greg had scoliosis, a curvature of the spine. It was not uncommon in children with arm discrepancies. There followed several visits with his orthopaedic surgeon, Dr. Steve Tredwell at BC Children's Hospital in Vancouver. It was felt Greg could not wear a back brace, which was a common form of treatment. Surgery was serious and would leave Greg with rods in his back and a further limitation in his ability to bend and reach. Dr. Tredwell had researched a new experiment being done at the University of California, Los Angeles. The plan was to apply a device, called a scolitron, onto Greg's back for twelve hours each night while he was sleeping. Each night at bedtime we applied an electrode on the top and the bottom of his curve and plugged him into an electrical circuit. There would be impulses every few seconds. The theory was that this would strengthen the muscles and correct the curvature. The reality was it did not work. We do not remember Greg ever complaining of this intrusive treatment he endured for many weeks.

* * *

Greg had an appointment to see Dr. Tredwell and to discuss what would happen next in his treatment. More X-rays and lung expansion tests were performed. Not only had the degree of his curve increased dramatically, but the lung function tests also indicated that there was actually pressure on his left lung and on his heart from the curve. He had grown several inches in a short time and this would explain the rapid progression. There was no other avenue left; surgery would have to be done.

We came home to pack and wait for a call that time had been "booked" in the operating room. It was only days until all four of us were on our way to Vancouver.

Greg was admitted a few days before his surgery. There was a protocol to be followed. He would meet a girl who had the same surgery performed by Dr. Tredwell. She would assure us that it was a long road but, like her, Greg would be pain free and able to walk several days after surgery. He would also spend hours each day and an overnight on a stryker frame prior to his surgery. It was the bed he would be on immediately following the surgery. He would actually be like "filling" in a sandwich. When it was time to be turned the top would be put on and two nurses would "flip" him from front to back and later from back to front.

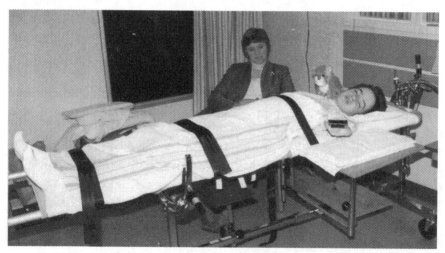

Dr. Tredwell had concerns about the surgery; not only had Greg's curve increased, but it was now a double or S-curve. The doctors would straighten the spine to relieve the pressure on Greg's heart and lung before they brought him out of the anaesthetic long enough to see if he could move his legs. The problem was that in order to accomplish this correction, Greg might be paralyzed from that vertebrae, meaning he would not be able to walk. It was one of the longest days of our life awaiting news from the operating room about Greg's progress. The good news was they were able to correct the curve enough to take the pressure off the vital organs without damage to the spinal cord but not enough to straighten Greg's back. He was left with a curve even with the Herrington rods.

During his hospitalization, we were approached about meeting with Variety, the Children's Charity, for his prosthetic costs. From 1982 until he turned nineteen this organization covered all expenses excluded by our medical plan.

The surgery was over and the next chapter in his life had begun.

* * *

Throughout junior high school and high school, Greg remained very committed to the band program playing various instruments. He won a scholarship to a summer program playing the vibraphone. He tried the slide trombone, playing with his feet, and he continued to entertain with his drumming expertise.

Sports remained a very important part of his life. He was manager of the junior boys' basketball team. At that time, Glen was curling and Greg had decided he wanted to join the same program. Mo determined that it was time he had a "heart to heart" talk with Greg that there were some things that he would not physically be able to do and curling was one of those options. Greg thought he should be able to try out for the team. We called the coach and asked if she would mind telling Greg that it was not possible for him to curl. We had a phone call after Greg's first lesson that she didn't know why not!! Greg curled for one season and seemed satisfied that he had accomplished that task!

* * *

After his back surgery, Greg was unable to ski for two years. He missed the thrill and the independence that the mountain offered. When he was able to resume, he did so with fervour. He competed with the disabled ski team and brought home gold medals from most every event he entered. One particular occasion stands out in my memory. It had been a week-long championship at Whistler Mountain.

Mo and I had arrived for the final two days. As always, we were very proud of his accomplishments. As he spoke to the crowd to accept his medal, he pretended that he was receiving an Academy Award. He wanted to thank the members of the Academy and to thank his parents for helping him to achieve such greatness! He had everyone in tears of laughter. His skill was not to be denied but his enjoyment of the sport and of his fellow skiers was most important.

* * *

The orthopaedic team from BC Children's Hospital approached Greg to ask if he would be interested in speaking to an international paediatric prosthetic convention being held in Vancouver in 1986. It was to be a ten-minute dialogue about wearing a prosthetic limb. Weeks before the conference I would ask Greg if he had started on his notes for the presentation. Ever the procrastinator, he would say "soon." The day arrived and he and I were on our way to Vancouver when he admitted to me that living for seventeen years with the subject he is about to speak on does not require notes!

The ten-minute presentation ended after one hour and the program for the remainder of the day was now behind schedule. Questions from doctors and prosthetists from around the world were unending. The one comment that made me aware that he has always known what was best for him was when he told the delegation that they must always pay attention to the request of the child, not the parent, not the doctor and not the prosthetist. There was applause and so many thanks from so many people. Once again he had made us proud. We have learned so much from this young man!

* * *

I should address the fact that Greg and Glen were also very typical boys. There were certainly moments when I wondered if I could cope with some of their antics! Then those moments would pass and they would do something that I could marvel at and say "yes, these are my sons!"

* * *

In 1986 the Provincial Games for the Disabled were held in Nanaimo. Mila Mulroney, the wife of Brian Mulroney, then Prime Minister of Canada, was a guest of the organizing committee. Greg had been very involved working for the organization. One sunny afternoon, the official opening of the games, my Mom was attending. Suddenly Greg was in front of her to introduce the Prime Minister's wife to his Grandma, a very proud moment for her.

* * *

Greg graduated from high school in 1987. He enrolled in college in Vancouver in September. Early in November we had a call that he had decided to quit school. We were shocked and frightened for him. We knew he needed an education. We also had to tell him that we would not financially support him if he were not going to continue his education.

He had employment as an instructor on Grouse Mountain. It was interesting that there was a need for an instructor who could not use poles. Several weeks later when Mo went over to ski with him for the day, he learned that Greg was the teacher of choice for beginners, both children and adults. A year later, at Christmas, Greg gave us a video starring him and filmed by a friend on his Mountain. It is an amazing epic of why he needed that year to be free of books and routines and to be able to enjoy living. At

the end of the video, he tells us that he would like to return to school. We were all delighted!

* * *

I should mention that summer saw Greg with employment at a local marina as a caretaker. He lived on a small boat. There he acquired another lifelong passion, sailing. I would tell friends that Greg was amazing and I was envious as he was suntanned year-round from skiing all winter and sailing all summer. I would imagine that would be a dream he might still have.

* * *

In 1992 Greg did a university semester on safari in Kenya. When the semester was complete, Greg stayed in Africa for several weeks. He has photos standing on the equator as well as photos of his arrival on the summit of Mt. Kilimanjaro. He returned to Canada with many stories and memories to share.

* * *

For his final year, Greg transferred to the University of Winnipeg and received his Bachelor of Science majoring in Climatology. Because there was no employment readily available, he called home to tell us he had seen a posting for a teaching opportunity in Warsaw, Poland, and that he had applied.

In July of 1994 he left for Warsaw on a one-year contract to teach Geography and English to International Baccalaureate students at a private high school. He would renew his contract for a second year. We went to visit him in that second year. It was a very different culture and lifestyle from Canada. He loved taking us to the vistas he had seen and to meet his friends. He was obviously enjoying the European way of life.

* * *

In 1997 Greg married Monika while they were on vacation in Canada from Poland. Veronika was born in 1998 and Karolina in 2003 in Warsaw. After Greg saw the first ultra sound of Veronika he was anxious to tell us that they had been able to see two arms and ten fingers. Years later I would tell this to one of his doctors. He shared with me that for Greg, who knew the hurt that can come with living with a physical challenge, this was indeed a wonderful sight.

* * *

In 2002 Greg obtained his MA in Sociology from Lancaster University in England. He is currently writing his PhD dissertation on Intercultural Management in Central and Eastern Europe. He has written extensively on the subject in academic journals.

* * *

Greg has a drivers licence both from Canada and from Europe. He is also the proud owner of a small sailboat.

At this time, Greg is living and working in Manchester, England. He is an advisor with the Greater Manchester Education Authority and an inter-cultural consultant assisting western business people in other countries.

He and Monika have divorced.

* * *

While doing some searching when I decided to write this journal, I came across an autobiography Greg had written in grade seven. With his blessings I can quote from it.

In a tired but excited voice she asked, "is it a Colleen or a Gregory?" "It's a healthy, brown hair, blue eyed Gregory" replied Dr. Nuyens. "But there is one thing I should tell you before you see your baby"

"What?" my Mother asked in a terrified voice.

"Your baby boy has two very small hands each with only one finger. We're not sure about one of them but the other he will never be able to use" replied Dr. Nuyens in a regretful voice.

Then a nurse brought me into my Mother's room and she saw me, and at that minute she knew that she would do everything she could to make my life as good as possible by getting me the best prostheses for my arms and all the best equipment for my handicap. My Dad was there and he had already seen me and he thought the same thing. When we all left to let my Mother get some rest, she looked out the window and saw boys playing football and she started to cry. Between two sobs she said "He'll never be able to catch a ball."

And from grade one:

In this year I met somebody with no arms that manages very well. His name is Alvin Law. He can play instruments and use a typewriter. Alvin plays the drums and the trombone. He plays the drums by sitting on a high stool and holding the sticks in his feet. The trombone is clamped onto the side of a chair and he moves the trombone with his feet. He can also swim and use a pocket camera. I think seeing all that Alvin could do with his feet made me feel that by the time I was 15 I would be able to do almost anything anybody else could.

This year I joined the Manitoba Riding for the Disabled. They had a good poem written by John Anthony Davies.

Thank God for Showing Me the Way

I saw a boy who couldn't walk
Sit on a horse and laugh and talk
Then ride it through a field of daisies
And yet he could not walk unaided.

I saw a child no legs below
Sit on a horse and make it go
Through wood of green and places he had never been
To sit and stare, except from a chair.

I saw a child who could only crawl,
Mount on a horse and sit up tall
Then put it through degrees of paces
And laugh at the wonder in our faces.

I saw a child born in strife
Take up and hold the reins of life
And that same child was heard to say
Thank God for showing me the way.

Greg's autobiography brought back some amazing memories. It will be wonderful for him to share with his daughters!

* * *

When I told Glen that I wanted to write this journal he encouraged me. Some weeks later, when we were visiting, he asked if I would like to read the paper he had written as part of his MBA application in 1999. With his blessing I am able to share with you from his paper entitled "Influences That Have Shaped Who I Am Today."

My younger brother, who has also been a vital link to our family bond, has had a more significant influence on my life than he will ever know. Greg was born without arms — a disability, which has always seemed to cause more problems for those around him than for Greg himself. A friend once asked me if it had been difficult growing up with a brother who had no arms; I eventually replied that Greg was my only brother and that I couldn't say growing up with him had been "difficult" because I had nothing to compare it to. Helping to button his shirts, tie his shoes and carry his books after school was just something that seemed normal to me because it had always been that way. Even Greg felt his circumstances were far less serious than onlookers presumed them to be, and over the years he has simply done his best to carry on as though nothing was any different for him than for anyone else. He has been involved in competitive equestrian events and is a certified downhill ski instructor.

He continues to prove to the world that despite his limitations, he is able to adapt to any challenges which come his way. I thank him for the inspiration he has provided over the years.

Glen and Greg — we are extremely proud of both of you!!

MIKE

Four days after Greg was born in 1969 in Ottawa, Mike arrived in Vancouver. He was the fourth child for my brother George. After Sean died in 1963 they had a son born in 1964 and a daughter in 1965. Kevin and Kelly were very healthy children. There was no reason to think that Mike would have any health issues.

Shortly after Sylvia weaned Mike from breast milk, they would fear that *acrodermatitis enteropathica* might return to haunt their lives. Mike started to develop skin problems and frequently experienced diarrhea. Doctors soon diagnosed Mike with the same affliction that had taken Sean's life.

Mike was frequently hospitalized. The La Leche League was notified of the need for breast milk and family and friends began an on-call system to travel and collect breast milk from many mothers who were eager to help.

* * *

The good news was that it had been discovered that a medication called entrovioform was being heralded as a "cure" for the disease, supplying the zinc that was missing in Mike's system.

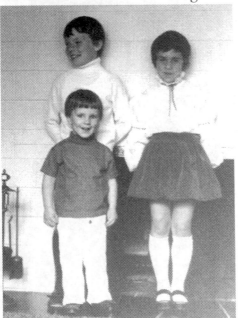

He seemed to do well on the medication. His skin cleared and he was able to tolerate and absorb food. It was some time later that his parents began to notice that when he was reading or watching TV he was always extremely close and they thought that perhaps his eyes needed testing. Sometimes when the other kids would see something of interest, Mike did not join in the conversation; perhaps he had not seen it.

With investigation, it was determined that Mike's vision was severely affected. What transpired in the weeks and months to follow was that medical expertise would acknowledge that the entrovioform he was taking had caused optic nerve damage. He had irreversible legal blindness caused by the medication. He was four years old. Entrovioform would later be removed from the market because it caused blindness!

* * *

Mike needs to take zinc sulfate daily for the rest of his life. His vision problems were researched and an alternate zinc medication was recommended by Dr. Bill Carr, his paediatrician in Nanaimo. His ophthalmologist, Dr. Richard Bowen, would research and complete a paper on the link between entrovioform and optic nerve damage, focusing on Mike.

Current medical literature says, "patients with *acrodermatitis enteropathica* uniformly respond to zinc therapy with a 100% survival rate."

* * *

During junior and senior high school, we all resided in Nanaimo. Greg and Mike were in the same grade. Mike was also very involved with sports and with the band program. He played the saxophone. He skied but his love was in the swimming pool. He became not only a competitive swimmer but also an Olympian!

* * *

The Paralympic Games in 1984 were in Long Island, New York. Mike came home with four Gold and two Silver Medals. In 1988 he would win nine Gold Medals in Seoul, Korea. His final

Olympic competition in 1992 in Barcelona, Spain, would see him return to Canada with four Gold and one Silver Medal. The family and Canada are very proud of his accomplishments.

In 2006 Mike was inducted into The Terry Fox Hall of Fame, "a permanent recognition of outstanding Canadians who have made extraordinary contributions to enriching the quality of life for people with physical disabilities."

* * *

One of the interesting memories of these two cousins was when they turned sixteen, the age in BC that you qualify to obtain a driver's licence. They decided that there really was no reason why together they couldn't accomplish the feat. After all, Greg could see the road that Mike could not and Mike could steer the car where Greg might not be able to!

* * *

They both carried the torch for the 1986 Provincial Games for the Disabled when they were held in Nanaimo.

* * *

When I asked Mike if I could include his story in my journal his response was "absolutely." He shared some of his achievements with me.

I was a motivational public speaker for nine years starting in 1988. I started with clubs like Rotary. I then joined the "Esteem Team" which is an athlete's speaker's bureau out of Burnaby, BC. Our focus was to address the youth of BC and Alberta regarding peer pressure, decision making, sports and other positive messages. I then spent some time speaking to corporations and non-profit organizations on motivation and teamwork.

Mike is presently a bank manager with the Royal Bank in Vancouver. He is married and has three very active, healthy, happy young sons. He has done well!

BLAKE

Sometime after we moved from Winnipeg to Nanaimo in 1980, I decided to do a "creative writing" course at the local college. I did one short course with one major assignment. I have not thought about the course again until I had the dream of doing this journal.

This is the writing project I did for that course and best tells the story of the next incredible young man I would meet on my life journey.

BLAKE — A Special Young Man

Probably one of the most "memorable" people I ever met and who, I'm sure, I will ever meet was a young man in Winnipeg.

When our family moved to Winnipeg in 1973 we began to slowly meet the neighbours — and what great neighbours they all proved to be in the months and years to follow. Across the street were the Smiths, an old time Manitoba family where both parents had been born and raised in a nearby small town. They had three children — two of whom we would meet soon after our arrival and who quickly became friends with our two sons. The third child — a young man even then — touched all of our lives as a very special person.

Blake was fourteen when we met. He was born a twin. His brother had died shortly after birth and his Mother tells the story that it was only a few days later that she believed Blake was not "normal." It took several weeks for doctors to confirm that Blake did suffer from cerebral palsy — a disease usually caused from brain damage due to lack of oxygen at birth.

The family had spent years of trying to do the best that therapy could do for the spasticity and contractures that Blake's weak muscles fought to control. It had been to no avail. Blake resided in his custom wheelchair and needed total care. His only responses to our world were a few audible sounds and some spastic movements whenever he was excited. The most important part of Blake's presence was his eyes. In his large blue eyes Blake had more responses and personality than most of us have in our entire being. He could literally talk and make you listen with his eye expression.

We became friends over the years — Blake and his family and our family.

He began his school career the year after we met. It became a very important part of his existence and a change in his family's life. For the first time Blake's Mother had a reprieve from the constant concern of being a mentor day and night. It gave her free time to become a more independent person — something that she had missed over the years. And how Blake loved school!

He had his usual school boy routine in the morning. Awakened, washed, dressed, and fed by Mom, he was in his wheelchair and waiting for his bus pick-up by 8:15 each weekday. Particularly during the Manitoba winters, his school day was a family affair as either Dad or brother Todd would have to make sure a path was shovelled through the snow to make a track for the wheelchair to travel.

* * *

The other highlight of Blake's day was when his Father came home from his day at work. It was always a game with Dad calling "Where is Blake? Where could he be hiding?" and then the guttural sound from Blake would lead his Dad to the hiding spot and the sparkle in Blake's eyes would assure Dad that he was well and had had a good day.

Blake made repeated appearances at the local hospital as the years progressed. His lungs could not expand to full capacity and he would find it increasingly more difficult to breathe. With oxygen and medication his visit was usually of short duration and he would return home well and ready to confront a new day.

He was a favourite with all the nurses on the paediatric ward on those short visits. Very quickly the nurses learned to respect the entire family for their spontaneous care and concern for Blake. Such was their esteem that we approached Blake's family doctor to arrange for a "social admission" each year so that his family could enjoy a well-deserved vacation knowing that Blake would be well cared for.

After much discussion and advising, the following year saw the four Smiths off to Disneyland and Blake on his own holiday on the Paediatric ward. His room was decorated for his arrival in Disneyland motif so that he too was really on vacation. His eyes didn't glisten though — he had accepted the family decision—but he was lonely and this wasn't home!

We visited often while his family was away but it became more and more difficult to see those brilliant, twinkling eyes turn so sober and quiet. But once he was home again, his routine re-established and Mom's homemade meals prepared, it seemed to take only hours for the sparkle in those eyes to return.

After the initial severance with Blake his parents became more self reliant and because Todd and sister Lynda were now old enough to be vigilant in Blake's care, some of the responsibility could be shared. Blake loved those two — Todd for his quiet self-assurance and calming effect, Lynda for her sparkle and humour and love *of life. If Blake could have chosen his family from the multitudes, he could not have chosen a better foursome.*

In winter, Blake travelled only between home and school so he loved the spring and summer months. He would sit for hours in the backyard, protected from the mosquitoes by the gazebo. Constantly listening, he seemed to enjoy family company whether they were Mom and Dad's friends or Todd and Lynda's. Then those eyes would dance and invite someone to push his chair for a tour of the neighbourhood — and upon each neighbour he met on his journey he would bestow a gleam from his eye and in return would see a glisten in a neighbour's eye.

Autumn was probably a favourite time for most people in Winnipeg. It was a welcome relief from soaring temperatures and high humidity. Blake would have a new lustre in his eyes when his wheelchair would crunch over the fallen leaves. It was also time to resume his school career and he would seem anxious each fall to become reacquainted with friends at school.

Christmas approached and became the highlight of early winter. Snow and multi-coloured lights attracted Blake as they did us all. On Christmas Eve, the jingle of bells and the mirth of laughter could always be heard approaching Blake's home shortly after dinner as Santa arrived. Blake was often hesitant — a year between visits was time to forget a face — but slowly you could see a flicker of recognition and then the eyes would glow as Santa would leave a stocking filled with trinkets from the local Police Department. No one seemed to know who Santa's helper on Christmas Eve really was and who encouraged his return each year, but we all came to rely on the excitement and the inevitable jingle of bells and chuckles of laughter at sunset on December 24th.

After the New Year, most everyone would settle in for the long cold Winnipeg winter and would see each other only on home visits and talk about spring. As is inevitable, 1980 being no exception, spring did indeed follow winter and with it all the hopes and dreams the new season nurtured. Blake looked forward to an occasional jaunt about the neighbourhood. It was a good feeling to see Blake as his appearance usually heralded that true spring weather was here to stay.

Because the school vacation was extended over the Easter weekend that year of '80 our family decided to use it to an advantage and enjoy a few days away from home. The Smiths invited us for a bon voyage dinner before we departed. Blake seemed to sense our excitement as his eyes darted from one to the other. We planned on leaving early the following day so we bade farewell shortly after dinner.

With a quick kiss on Blake's cheek we wished him a Happy Easter and he in response glowed — and unknowingly to many — wished us a happy vacation. We finished packing and left on schedule the following morning.

We had an enjoyable drive through southern Manitoba and settled into our poolside room looking forward to a relaxing few days. How our boys relished the pool being just outside the door!

On Easter Sunday the ring of the telephone jarred our sleep early in the morning. As I rolled over to answer, assured it was a wrong number — I was stunned, first at the silence and then at the sound of Blake's Dad. He was sorry to wake us but needed to share his awesome tidings — Blake had just passed away. His eyes were closed but that special twinkle and that very special young man would never be forgotten.

We were on our way before dawn for our return to Winnipeg. As we drove toward a most glorious sunrise one could not help but think of another very special young man who had also left his family and friends at Easter time. Such bewildering news we had received on such a beautiful, bright day and yet we could feel both sadness and joy. We had lost such a special friend but as we remembered the moments of our friendship with Blake, each of us knew we were better people for having had the pleasure of knowing this young man.

I received an A for this assignment, although I am sure it was more for the content than for the actual composition!

* * *

We have remained friends with the Smiths. They still live in the same house in Winnipeg. Todd has a BA in Computer Science, is married and lives in Victoria. Lynda has her BSc. in Nursing. She works in the Neonatal Intensive Care Unit in Winnipeg. She is married and has a daughter and son.

MICHAEL

In 1988 I was working casual shifts on the paediatric ward in Nanaimo.

As much as I didn't enjoy the way politics had found its way into nursing, I did enjoy the challenges of my chosen profession. I also valued the friendship of my colleagues. It was a superb group of talented professionals I had the privilege of working with in those years.

During the autumn of 1988, a youngster was admitted with a variety of vague symptoms. He had been born at the hospital in September of 1987. His parents would give a history of on-going vomiting and peculiar movements. The staff would consider the "first time anxious parent" malady. Eventually we would learn that Michael did suffer from a movement disorder, that he was *microcephalic* — having an abnormally small head and an underdeveloped brain. He also had ongoing problems retaining his food.

* * *

Early in 1990 I heard of a new nursing program in our province. It was a paediatric respite program for families facing challenges caring for medically fragile children. A registered nurse would be assigned for a varied number of hours each week depending on the needs of the child and of the family.

I applied for a position on the team and I was accepted. The first family I met was Michael's! The name had not seemed familiar on the information I had been given, but as soon as Michael's Mom opened the door we recognized each other. It was good — we knew and liked each other!

Michael's needs had really increased. He was now being tube fed through a "button" into his stomach. His movement disorder had intensified. He was on medication to try and control the seizure-type of movements. They were not often effective. He literally needed twenty-four-hour care. His parents were exhausted and his Mom was pregnant with the baby due shortly.

Two other registered nurses were also employed. One was already a friend, Jan, and the other, Elizabeth, quickly became one. We were a team with Michael's parents and his grandparents. He was a challenging boy most days but his friends could see the difference we were making in his family's life. When Lindsay arrived as a healthy sister in May of 1990, we made it possible for Mom and Dad to spend some quality time with her while we cared for Michael.

* * *

Michael's medical needs became ever more serious and frightening to all of us. His parents stayed at the hospital with him whenever he was admitted; the nurses on the ward just could not spend the time with him that was necessary.

His parents and I discussed what would be most helpful to them in the challenges they had just getting through each day with a new baby and the constant care required by Michael.

We approached his social worker with the Ministry for Social Services about the possibility of Mo and I being able to bring Michael to our home for respite, thus giving his Mom and Dad a chance to actually sleep for an entire night! The Ministry wasn't sure if that were possible but said they would look into it. Some weeks later there was a meeting with Michael's medical team, his social worker, his parents and me. In order for Michael to come to our home, we would have to become foster parents. His "real" parents did not have a problem with the designation! His social worker, Mike, seemed pleased that we had a team that was looking forward to caring for Michael and supporting one another.

Our home at that time was a wonderful old heritage home and Mo now had his framing shop in the basement. It seemed an ideal situation for taking on this new adventure. If I needed help with Michael, we had a system where three thumps on the floor indicated that I needed his assistance.

Our den was turned into "Michael's Room" for several days each month. We enjoyed his company and often he would give me an adrenalin rush with his medical challenges. It was also rewarding to see the difference the plan was making to his family's life.

* * *

Glen was living in Japan that year and for Michael's birthday in September he sent an official Tokyo Giants baseball uniform. It would be the only baseball uniform he would ever wear. Years later, Michael's Mom returned the uniform to Glen for his son Jonathan.

* * *

In December of 1992 we had Michael at our home for a few days before Christmas. His parents were able to join in some of the season's festivities and share with Lindsay her holiday excitement. They came for Michael on Christmas morning and shared the wonder of the day with our family before they left to spend the day with their family.

On New Year's Eve I had a call from Elizabeth who was with Michael at his home for the evening. She had called for his parents, as he was not well. He was taken to the local hospital where I went to see him. His condition was critical and he was transferred by helicopter to BC Children's Hospital in Vancouver. I went to visit him there on January 5th. His condition was not improving.

On January 9th we had a phone call from his Grandmother that Michael and his Mom were "coming home" to Nanaimo by helicopter. Dad would follow on the ferry. His Grandma and Lindsay and I were waiting at the hospital for him to arrive. We had his hospital room ready with his favourite comforter. We hoped it would look a little like home.

When Michael, his Mom and his doctor arrived, I realized the gravity of the situation. Michael had come home to die. An hour after he arrived he would leave us. His Mom was able to hold him until the end. His Dad was still on the ferry. When he arrived at the hospital I remember him sharing with me that he knew exactly when Michael had died. He was on the ferry looking out at the sea and there was a starburst around the sun as it set in the sky looking toward Nanaimo.

* * *

Michael's funeral was on January 14th, 1993. I had written a letter and given it to his parents. They asked if it could be used as his eulogy. I was honoured but told them I would not be able to read it. The

Minister at his service would read it. With their permission, I add it to my journal.

Dear Michael:

I have thought a lot in the past few days of the best way to say goodbye. Today I decided I would write a letter to you.

You are such a special young man who chose to visit us here on earth for five plus years and take us on an adventure — and what an adventure it has been. You took us to the highest peaks with your smiles and your giggles — and you took us into the deepest valleys with your medical emergencies — we all went down into those valleys with you — but you were always surrounded with so much love from so many friends and that love somehow seemed to be the wind beneath your wings. Time after time you led us back up to the mountain peak and gave us more smiles and so much love.

From your first breath to your very last breath you have been Mommy's boy — her Smiley Joe — do you remember all those special cuddles and tickles until you would smile and she would say "that's my Smiley Joe"? And always you were Daddy's buddy — remember how he would roll you over and over on the floor and make you happy when you weren't feeling great?

Lindsay will always remember you as love, Michael — she has seen and felt more love because of you than some of us will know in a much longer lifetime than yours. And if you could have chosen your Grandparents, you could not have made a better choice than the ones you have — they will miss you so much, young man.

We all know how much you wanted to stay here with us. We want you to know that we love you very much for staying as long as you did, but we understand how tired you must be. Rest in peace little Buddy — you have earned that right. I know our love has been beneath your wings to get you to those mountain peaks. We know that it is your turn now and that you will be the wind beneath our wings to help us go on without you — we love you Michael — we will miss you so much.

Trudy and Larry had chosen an awesome selection of music for the service. The one I remember as being the most heart-rending was written by Dolly Parton and entitled "I Will Always Love You."

If I should stay
Well, I would only be in your way
And so I'll go, and yet I know
That I'll think of you every step of the way
And I will always love you.
I will always love you…

And I hope life, will treat you kind
And I hope that you have all
That you ever dreamed of
Oh, I do wish you joy
And I wish you happiness
But above all this
I wish you love
I love you, I will always love you

It seemed the words were written for Michael to send to the ones who loved him.

* * *

In the weeks that followed Michael's death, his Mom would share with me that she thought it was somehow easier to get through each day thinking that he was on one of his sleepovers at our home. Lindsay would ask if it were time to bring Mikey home thinking he was at our place.

* * *

Michael's parents are divorced but they both still live in Nanaimo. Lindsay is a delightful young lady who excels in school and in gymnastics.

* * *

Michael was never given a diagnosis — his Mom told me when I spoke to her about my journal that it was and still is a mystery what his affliction was.

* * *

Months after his death, Michael's three nurses would look at real estate with thoughts of opening a respite home for kids like Michael. We had decided it would be called Michael's Place. Parents would "book" a theme room for respite. We found a building that would be perfect. Jan, who was the "designer" amongst us, had plans for Minnie's Room, Pooh's Room, Cinderella's Room — our imaginations were endless! It was a great plan, but it never materialized! I have often thought we should have pursued the dream — it was and still is a much-needed therapy in our society. Years later, in Vancouver, a paediatric hospice opened called Canuck Place and is a blessing for those families living in that area.

LUCAS

Some months after Michael's death I had a call from his social worker, Mike. I had told him that I didn't think I would be able to endure the emotions of supporting another family. He informed me that this particular young fellow he would like me to meet had different challenges!

So, in the spring of 1993, I met Lucas. He was born in Vancouver in July of 1990. His family was planning on moving to Nanaimo. They needed ongoing nursing respite.

Lucas had been diagnosed shortly after birth with *Opitz G Syndrome*. It is a genetic condition that affects several structures along the midline of the body. The most common features are wide-spaced eyes and defects of the esophagus, causing breathing problems and difficulty swallowing. It in itself was a major disability but he also had a bilateral cleft lip and palate. Additionally, he also underwent surgery in the first days of his life for a congenital diaphragmatic hernia, and had several surgeries to try and repair the opening in his trachea or windpipe. He was unable to eat or drink due to this opening. His voice box was involved as well. Doctors commented on how unusual it was to have so many complex abnormalities in one child, each being a major problem of a life-threatening nature.

It was nine months before Lucas was able to leave the hospital. The remarkable news was that, despite his multiple physical challenges, he was developmentally normal and reached milestones at an appropriate age.

* * *

Lucas had a tracheotomy and was fed by a gastrostomy tube into his stomach. His Mom gave a history of a rocky beginning to Lucas's life but the family had an amazing will for him to survive. One of his doctors from BC Children's Hospital said that it was an incredible story for a child to overcome so many serious medical conditions and survive. It was a credit to his family and to the fighter that Lucas proved to be over the years.

It had been years since I had nursed anyone with a tracheotomy but the team that taught those of us who would do the respite program for Lucas was great.

* * *

The nurses did mostly nights in Lucas's home and two of us attended preschool with him. I soon realized that Lucas was one very clever boy. The classroom had a two-way mirror. In theory we would be able to observe him for any medical needs while he was unaware that he was being watched. Within days, if he wanted us to see one of his projects or to share a new friendship, he would saunter over to the "mirror" and give it a tap to get our attention. So much for the theory of his nurses being invisible!

* * *

Early in 1994 Lucas became our foster-child so that he could come to our home for respite, much as Michael had done. We so enjoyed his company. He was a trial grandchild for us. We spent many hours at the playgrounds and at the beaches. One of his favourite places was a train

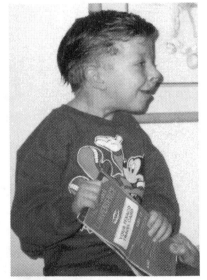

museum a few miles from our home. I'm not sure which came first, the train museum or *Thomas the Tank Engine* videos, but we were all enamoured with trains!

* * *

Greg and Lucas had a special bond. Greg was living in Vancouver so when Lucas came to our home for "sleepovers" he would sleep in Greg's room. If Greg happened to be home on the same weekend, he would have to sleep in Glen's room. Lucas loved that he was given priority! Some mornings when I would go upstairs they had already started their day with stories and giggles. Greg once told me how much he enjoyed Lucas's company and that it reminded him of such a great period in his own life.

Glen remembers Lucas as a character, and for sure he was! A lovable, huggable, clever, mischievous and fun-to-have-around character.

* * *

In the autumn of 1994 Lucas was admitted to BC Children's Hospital. The doctors thought he might be able to breathe without his tracheotomy. The team would teach him how he was to inhale and exhale when the tube was removed from his throat. Often it was not successful on the first attempt and it would be reinserted for a period of time. Lucas could have taught the course. His tube was removed and he took a deep breath and continued as though he had never been intubated some four-and-a-half years earlier. He was very proud of himself and we were very proud of him!

Without his tracheotomy his life was much more comfortable. Another milestone on his long medical road was completed. The dramatic change for Lucas and for his family is that he no longer required respite! They could begin to know life without nurses in their home. We had done our job; Lucas had graduated from our care.

* * *

We have kept in touch occasionally over the years since. His parents are divorced. Lucas lives with his Mom and sister Kelsey at Shawnigan Lake — the village where I grew up! His Dad lives in Nanaimo.

His Mom shares that Lucas has had some forty-nine anaesthetics in his eighteen years, including three recent facial surgeries.

Speaking with Lucas, he tells me that he will be graduating from Frances Kelsey School near Shawnigan Lake. He is taking mostly sciences this semester and his long-term plans will be to go on in biology or genetics. He will do well wherever his path leads him. He, too, is an amazing young man!

* * *

Another remarkable coincidence is that his school is named after Frances Kelsey who grew up on a farm near Shawnigan Lake. She attended McGill University in Montreal and obtained her degree in Pharmacology. She went on to acquire her PhD in the United States and was employed by the FDA. She is credited with keeping the drug Thalidomide from being sold in the US. It caused *phocomelia* (Greg's diagnosis). Ten thousand kids in forty-six countries (including Canada) were estimated to be born with deformities as a consequence of Thalidomide use. I attended the opening of the school in 1995 and actually met Dr. Kelsey.

JENELLE

Some people come into our lives and quickly go.
Some stay awhile, leave footprints on our hearts.
And we are never, ever the same.

Flavia Weedn

It was a late Christmas gift in 1994 when our tattered Angel came into our life and into our hearts. Jenelle was born in Vancouver on Sept. 24th, 1994. Her family was from Nanaimo but complications during her Mom's pregnancy and concern for Jenelle's health had indicated her arrival should be close to BC Children's Hospital. It had been a wise decision.

Jenelle was diagnosed moments after her arrival with *Cornelia de Lange Syndrome*. Her chances of surviving birth or the immediate hours following were minimal. Eventually, she was transferred to the local hospital in Nanaimo. After several team meetings with family, health and social services ministries, Jenelle was sent home; the family was assured that they would receive any help they required for the short time that Jenelle was expected to survive.

Again we received a call from Mike, "our" social worker and now friend, that there was a family he thought would benefit from my experience. I told him that we had "retired" from the emotional roller coaster we had shared with him. I could almost see him smiling as he said he would wait to hear from me!

Our Christmas letter sent to friends in 1994 reads "I am still working with the Paediatric Nursing Respite Program and willingly admit it has been the most gratifying position I have ever held... We will be home for Christmas this year — hosting twenty-one of my family for Christmas dinner."

And so, with a busy Christmas season finished, I thought I should check in to see if the Ministry had found support for the family they had mentioned.

* * *

On January 5th, 1995, I was informed by Mike that he had been waiting for my call! Arrangements were made for me to meet Jenelle and her family.

It had been such a remarkable fact that of all the "special" kids in my life, they had all been boys. I was quite looking forward to meeting this little girl, Jenelle. On January 11th, Mo's birthday, I was introduced to an Angel.

Jenelle was sitting in an infant seat, her colour indicated she certainly had heart and/or lung issues. She had a nasogastric tube — a tube through her nose to her stomach for feeding a child who is unable to suck or swallow. She was so very tiny. And the most amazing feature for me was that her arms were almost identical to Greg's! I had a feeling of déjà vu. Was it meant to be that I was being introduced to this family? Was there a higher authority that wanted me to continue my involvement with these extraordinary children?

I was introduced to Jenelle's parents, to her eight-year-old brother Jamie and three-year-old sister Jenni Lynn. Her Grandmother lived very close by and spent much of her day helping out. There was some support in place for assisting the family. Jenelle's needs were very complex and the Ministry felt they would like me on board to not only share the physical care for Jenelle but to give encouragement and comfort to the family. She had already been diagnosed as palliative care with only a brief time expected here on earth.

I returned home to share the image of this precious wee girl with Mo. I think he momentarily wondered if we could embrace yet another challenge. I assured him he should just meet her and he would be in love again!

* * *

I started to research *Cornelia de Lange Syndrome* — or as we would quickly come to learn *CdLS*. Dr. Cornelia de Lange, a Dutch paediatrician, described the collection of symptoms comprising the syndrome in 1933.

It is a multiple congenital anomaly syndrome, meaning it is present at birth. It is characterized by a distinctive facial appearance, pre-natal and post-natal growth deficiency, feeding difficulties, psychomotor delays, behavioural problems and associated malformations mainly involving the upper extremities. We quickly learned that Jenelle's arms were referred to as "Angel Wings" in the *CdLS* vocabulary. A child need not demonstrate each and every sign or symptom for the diagnosis to be made.

Jenelle had arrived here on earth weighing two pounds eleven ounces. She presented with most of the defining characteristics of *CdLS* including heart defects which seemed to be life threatening from a medical viewpoint. It was very difficult for her to suck — she did not seem to have the strength and would tire easily. If she was unable to swallow, she could aspirate the formula into her lungs. The doctors had asked the family to try and keep her very quiet and content, as crying would place an even greater stress on her heart. She had *microcephaly*, a very tiny head circumference with an underdeveloped brain.

* * *

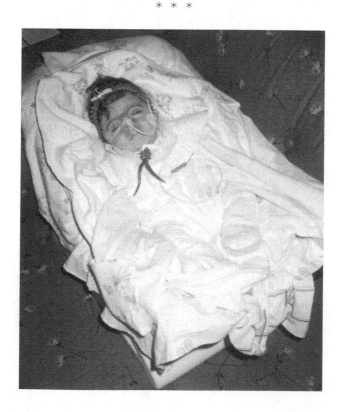

At three months, Jenelle weighed just less than five pounds. I joined the team already in place to give the family some much-needed support. Jenelle would be admitted frequently both to the hospital in Nanaimo and to BC Children's Hospital in Vancouver for ongoing assessment. The medical team did not give the family hope that Jenelle would ever be able to overcome her challenges and she remained palliative.

Jenelle had a nasogastric tube inserted so that she could obtain her nourishment and hopefully not aspirate and cause pneumonia. As is one of the quirks of *CdLS*, she had reflux and could aspirate even with the tube feeding method. More medications were added to her regime.

* * *

It wasn't long until Jenelle, her family, her social worker and Mo and I thought it possible we could have her visit our home to give her family a rest.

I will never forget the apprehension we felt at bringing this very small bundle of love with such incredible challenges into our home. I'm sure we didn't sleep those first few times she visited. Her voice was very quiet and very weak. Even then she had a most amazing smile.

* * *

The weeks turned into months and doctors seemed unable to explain why Jenelle was defying the odds. We were on vacation in September 1995 (her first birthday) when some bureaucrats decided that she was no longer to be classified as palliative. It should have been good news but in fact it meant that some of the family support would be withdrawn. I tried to advocate for the family but to no avail.

In our Christmas letter in 1995 I wrote "I (we!) have become more involved in the respite program and at this time have a most adorable fifteen-month-old Angel called Jenelle as an almost full-time house guest — she is palliative and although her family love her very much, her present care is more than they can cope with so we are enjoying her company."

* * *

Jenelle was hospitalized and diagnosed with congestive heart failure in January of 1996. Her nursing needs exceeded what her family was comfortable performing. So, after much discussion, we agreed that we would be her foster family with her full-time care and her biological family would be part of our respite team. We were reversing roles. It was certainly discussed that this would be short term as her life expectancy was still considered grave.

It was interesting. The family and friends who were supportive of our respite care for these kids thought, when they heard Jenelle was with us on a full-time plan, that we were quite mad! We would smile and say that life had been good to us and it felt good to be able to give back. We wanted to bestow on her all the love we could for the little time she had here on earth.

And so, the adventure of living with this little bundle sent from Heaven began!

* * *

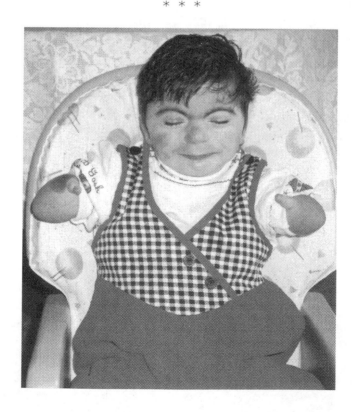

One of the first thoughts I had to make both Jenelle's life and those of us who would care for her more comfortable and indeed safer was to approach her medical team about a G-tube or Mickey button into her stomach in place of the nasogastric tube for her tube feedings. The team agreed, but was concerned about administering an anaesthetic to insert the G-tube. It was eventually decided that the quality of her life would be enhanced if the surgery were done. She tolerated the procedure well and for the first time we had a vision without tubes of the pixie face and extraordinary smile that is Jenelle.

* * *

Jenelle's room was our den. She slept most of the time. Her bed was a cradle that friends had given to us when Greg was born. We had loaned it many times to new babies. They had all been boys. Now we had our precious wee girl sleeping in it. She was always in her infant seat, as she had to remain elevated both for her heart and for her feeding regime.

Jenelle went for visits to her parents' home and would occasionally have a sleepover. We had remained friends with Michael's parents. He had been gone three years now and his Mom had expressed an interest in doing respite care for kids with special needs. I had discouraged her, thinking she needed a change from the concern that would always accompany these little people. Years later I knew why she needed to nurture these feelings. And so, Michael's family became our respite family, as we had been theirs. One day when we were picking Jenelle up, Michael's Dad told us that he had often wondered how they would be able to express their gratitude for the help we had been in their lives. He smiled and told us he would not have even dreamed it would be as foster parents for our Angel.

* * *

Jenelle had frequent doctor's appointments both in Nanaimo and in Vancouver. She had a multi-disciplinary team with most every specialty in the medical profession! It was wonderful for us to know her paediatrician in Nanaimo was Dr. Bill Carr. We knew him both from personal consults and from the other families with whom we had been involved. In Vancouver, at BC Children's Hospital, we met Dr. Jane Hailey, a paediatrician who would be the central part of Jenelle's medical team. She had been in the delivery room when Jenelle was born and the first to utter the diagnosis of *CdLS*. She would become a friend and an unwavering advocate of Jenelle's over the years.

We became almost daily visitors to the *CdLS* Foundation website. The information on the site is amazing. From that site, we also joined the international online support group of families with children afflicted with *CdLS*. Medical advice from the Scientific Advisory Council was returned hours after our questions were posted. Children and caregivers before us had accomplished the answers to everyday challenges in our life with Jenelle, and parents on the support group were more than pleased to share their experiences with us. These professionals and families came from around the world; it truly is an international organization.

* * *

During the ensuing years, when Jenelle was well, we had a routine that made our days very enjoyable. She loved to smile. She loved music, not only her children's songs but also Mo's classical music, particularly the violin. She could keep perfect time to the different beats. She also loved time in her exersaucer. Mo had attached a tambourine to the tray of the saucer and she would play it with the intensity of a concert musician. She loved to play, taking turns with different activities, but her favourite was alternating her "Angel wings" for Mo to kiss. I knew when I heard her giggles emanating from the den to the kitchen that she and Mo were having their special time! Mo still had his picture framing business downstairs in our home. When he came up for lunch or at the end of his business day he would knock on the wall, and whatever Jenelle was doing at that time she would turn toward the door with her biggest and best smile for her best friend.

* * *

One day we were shopping in a mall. Greg was home on a visit from Poland so he had joined Mo, Jenelle and me. We smiled at each other as two ladies gazed at Jenelle in the stroller and were staring at this unique little girl. Then their gaze shifted to Greg. The expression on their face was priceless. It would have been interesting to hear their conversation as they strolled off about these two individuals who looked so much alike. We were sure we could see Jenelle's smile as though she, too, knew what we were chatting about.

* * *

We had a cabin some twenty-minute drive and a short boat ride from our home. We purchased a life jacket for Jenelle and she seemed to enjoy the fresh air and quiet of spending time at the cabin with us in good weather.

She certainly had her health issues in those years, but as she would recover from each episode and return home from hospital, we would forget the past and enjoy each day and look forward to tomorrow.

* * *

During the summer of 2000, we left Jenelle with Elizabeth and Trudy. They would live at our home and share the care and responsibility of our Angel while we travelled to Europe with friends. Greg met us in Paris for a few days. One evening we were fortunate to attend an open-air concert under the Eiffel Tower. Andrea Bocelli, the amazing, blind Italian tenor was performing. Greg asked if I had ever imagined standing with him and his Dad in Paris listening to such a voice! The answer was a very simple one: No, not even in my dreams! Andrea sang a song I will never forget, "Time to Say Goodbye."

* * *

Jenelle started preschool at the local Child Development Centre in Nanaimo. There she was involved with Jane, her physiotherapist, with occupational therapy, with speech therapy and with her support worker and teachers. She was very quiet and her perpetual smile won everyone's heart.

As always with these special children, Jenelle taught that to be different was OK. Here was a little girl who was carried or in a stroller unable to walk…ever; unable to speak…ever; and only able to communicate in her own special way and only to those who would take the time to understand and appreciate her. Her smiles and giggles would melt the heart of most everyone we met.

* * *

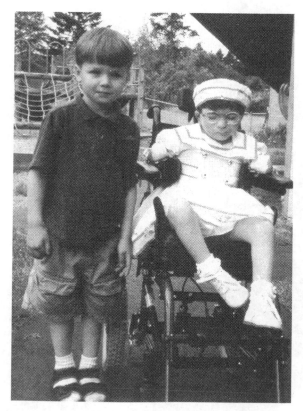

Her best childhood friend from her first year at preschool and through all her school years was an extraordinary young man named Angus. He told me early on in their friendship that he would always be Jenelle's protector. She had many friends in the course of her school years but Angus was the constant, always there to answer questions about her or for her.

Veronika, our granddaughter from Poland, became friends with Jenelle when she came to Canada to visit. I remember the year when Veronika was two and Jenelle six and how interesting it was to observe them together. Veronika actually weighed more than Jenelle! We have wonderful photos of the two, happy to be together. Veronika was always so understanding, patient and affectionate. They were buddies in a world of differences.

* * *

In June of 2001 Mo and I would accompany Jenelle to Costa Mesa, California, for an international conference on *Cornelia De Lange Syndrome*.

We flew from Nanaimo to California. She was such a good little traveller and was given many smiles from a variety of people both in the airports and on the plane.

We arrived at the Hyatt Hotel where the conference was to take place. It was an incredible sight in the main lobby. There we saw, for the first time, the amazing facial similarities we had read about. We really were part of a large family. We didn't initially see others with "Angel wings" and most were much more mobile than Jenelle. In her journal I wrote "she is definitely the cutest one here."

We had occasion to speak with one of the hotel employees who shared with us that the staff had been told of the nature of this Conference. They were given the option of whether they chose to work on this particular weekend. Some had declined and others, like this young man, had said he would be there as many hours as was necessary. For those who had said they would share their time with this odd looking group of special children there was a briefing. They had been told not to ask parents checking in if another family member had already arrived. The kids looked so much alike, it would have been easy to assume they were related. Indeed, we were part of a very special family!

* * *

The Conference was very busy, very educational and very interesting. The genetic research was so important to the medical advisory board from all over the world. Jenelle had blood taken to be a part of this study to try and find the *CdLS* gene, which they seemed so close to identifying.

There was a group of girl guides from the US that were able to take care of the *CdLS* kids while their families attended the workshops. Several years previously one of these girls had a sibling with *CdLS* and now this group travelled the world each year the Conference was held to perform this function. Jenelle spent one session with them but Mo was very happy to spend the hours with Jenelle while I absorbed as much as I could of the implications for Jenelle living with this syndrome.

During one of the sessions where all three of us attended, we were asked by the doctor how involved we were with the Deafblind Association. By this time we were aware that Jenelle had both vision and hearing impairments. She was wearing glasses and we attempted to introduce her to hearing aides. I told them we did not have such an organization in Canada. By the time we returned to Nanaimo there was an email from the doctor and from the Deafblind Association of BC! Jenelle was on their expedited list for a consult before she started school in September.

* * *

Mo had taken photos and diagrams of the way he had transformed the exersaucer to adapt to Jenelle's needs. There was a room designated as "show and tell" and many parents were interested in sharing his expertise. He also learned ways to adapt others ideas to make life for Jenelle more interesting.

* * *

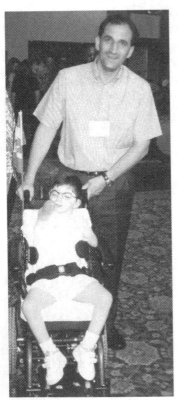

One of the great photos we have from the conference is of a geneticist from Italy with Jenelle. He had asked if he could take her photo as she was the first "text book" child he had met with the syndrome. Jenelle really did exhibit each of the criteria for *CdLS* but for a bowel abnormality called a "volvulus."

* * *

On the last day in Costa Mesa, the families were invited to be guests of Disneyland. A bus picked us up at the Hotel and delivered us. There, Disney Ambassadors met us. What an unbelievable afternoon we experienced. Jenelle met Pooh and his friends; she was introduced to Minnie and her friends. Not once did we or any of the families have to stand in line. She went on the "It's a Small World" ride. The music will always bring memories of sharing the ride with her.

It's a world of laughter, a world of tears
It's a world of hope and a world of fears
There's so much that we share
That it's time we're aware
It's a small world after all

We were escorted wherever we chose and treated like royalty. What an amazing end to add to our memories of the summer of 2001.

* * *

In September, Jenelle started in a grade one class. She had the same teacher as she had in Kindergarten. Her educational assistant, who would be with Jenelle one-on-one for her remaining school years, was

Gail. We all learned to appreciate and love Gail for her quiet-spoken, compassionate concern for Jenelle and, indeed, for us as well!

That autumn, Jenelle's physio introduced her to the Mulholland walker. In it she could stand with a pummel between her legs and a wide strap around her body. She had taken a few steps in it at home but one day we took it to school. Gail's note in her school journal that day says that at recess she had followed her classmates and walked the length of the concrete play area, some fifty feet! She walked shorter distances for awhile but for unknown reasons to us, decided that mobility was not on her agenda!

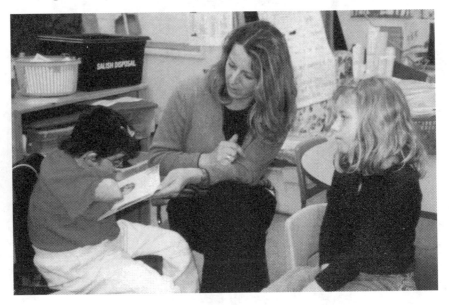

* * *

Jenelle tried hearing aides that autumn with very limited success. It was amazing how she could manipulate her head and shoulders and her Angel wing to remove them. We tried them off and on for several attempts but were never successful.

* * *

The new man in Jenelle's life was Al. He drove the school bus for the kids with disabilities. She was now in a custom wheelchair and accepted for transportation to and from school. I wasn't convinced that this was a good thing! For the first few days I would accompany her to school on the bus and then walk home. It didn't take long to realize that she was in very competent and kind hands travelling the short distance with Al. Like Gail, he would be Jenelle's driver for the remainder of her school years.

* * *

Jenelle spent her seventh birthday not feeling well. She was getting over pneumonia and further heart failure. She tired very easily. But one smile as she started to feel better and we all celebrated with her.

* * *

Jenelle had been approved for the Deafblind program in Nanaimo. Mo and Gail attended a workshop given by the group and were introduced to Gerald who would work with Jenelle for the next two years on her communication skills. One of the initial challenges Gerald felt was of importance was communication by "turn taking." We had a small piano, which Jenelle loved to play with her feet when she was sitting on the floor. Gerald sat on the floor with her. Jenelle would tinkle the keys; Gerald would tinkle the keys and then wait

71

for Jenelle to respond. It took very few sessions and the two of them were playing duets. Jenelle enjoying every minute of waiting for Gerald to take his turn. She was such a tease!

Our Christmas letter from 2001 reads

Jenelle, our precious foster daughter is now seven years old, in a grade one class, involved with the Deafblind Association for communication and, with the help of a wonderful T.A., is making progress which we had never expected. She has had a fairly good year health wise and still continues to make her medical experts shake their heads!

Jenelle spent Christmas that year with Rosalind and her family. They had been a part of our respite team for several months. It was the first Christmas she had not been with us. We were two days in Victoria spending Christmas with Jonathan, who had arrived on December 14th, our second grandchild and first grandson. We had a wonderful time but were anxious to get home to our Angel!

* * *

Over the years, Jenelle was very tolerant of Jonathan. He brought new sounds to our home as a baby, some crying, some cooing and loads of adoring comments from Grandparents. When he started crawling, he would often crawl over Jenelle as she was lying on the floor. She didn't protest although we sometimes wondered if she breathed a sigh of relief when he left! Glen always made sure he gave Jenelle her own special time with him. I would often marvel as I walked by her room and would see the two of them on the floor, Jenelle looking at Glen

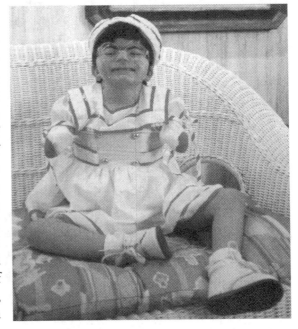

and he speaking ever so softly to her; it was a unique love and acceptance from his heart.

* * *

When she returned to school in January I had written in her school journal that she had been very quiet, sleeping for long periods, difficult to engage in activity and laughter. We were wondering if she was perhaps bored and missing her friends. Sure enough, in her notes from school, Gail had written that she was very alert and seemed very happy! There was also a drawing sent to us from Angus saying how much he had missed her.

* * *

We were told often by classmates, teachers, neighbours, friends, family and even strangers that Jenelle was somewhat of a fashion icon. It was such fun to dress her. I loved shopping for clothes and accessories for a girl; our granddaughters shared most of her wardrobe over the years, but Jenelle was our first lassie. She was like dressing a doll. She looked wonderful in pink. Her socks, hair clips and headbands matched her outfits! She had the most beautiful dark hair cut in a pixie style. Unlike others, she kept her clothes clean and looked as perfect when we changed her into her pajamas as she had when we dressed her to start her day!

We walked the seawall close to our home often. Jenelle had a hat to match most everything she wore. Many a passerby admired her and over the years she had her own circle of friends that we only saw on our trek along the ocean.

* * *

Jenelle's chest problems were becoming more frequent and more severe each time. She was missing a fair amount of school. And yet again, each time she recovered, we would forget the past and enjoy the days she was feeling well. She was now on Ventolin and Pulmicort, drugs to try and ease her breathing difficulties.

* * *

By April, 2002, Gerald, her facilitator from the Deafblind Association, felt that Jenelle, with Gail's help, was making great strides in communication. Jenelle was the only girl in a class with seven boys. One day I helped Jenelle to do an Awareness Day to teach the boys more about *CdLS* and how it impacted so many parts of Jenelle's life. In the afternoon, the boys gave the presentation to the Kindergarten children. Jenelle's teacher, Wendi, called me that evening to tell me how well the boys had listened and how well they had presented Jenelle's life to their schoolmates.

* * *

In May, Jenelle was having increasing difficulty with chest congestion. She now had oxygen in her room and we used it frequently to ease her struggle to breathe without exertion. She required suctioning to clear her throat of thick mucus. We saw Dr. Sandor, her cardiologist at BC Children's Hospital. She now had fluid around her heart. Dr. Hailey would tell us that she felt Jenelle was "outgrowing" her heart capacity. She was started on steroids to see if that would improve the serious condition we were encountering. By the end of the month there had been little improvement in her condition. After an echocardiogram done in Nanaimo and a call placed to BC Children's Hospital, Jenelle and I were on our way to Vancouver by helicopter.

As would happen each time we left emergency en route to BC Children's Hospital, Mike, our incredible friend and social worker, would come (day or night!) to stay with Jenelle and me until the team of medical experts arrived to transport us. Mo would leave to get the next ferry so he could be at the hospital in Vancouver as soon as possible.

After eight days on the cardiac unit, Jenelle's health had improved enough that we could return home. I stayed in her room with her so it was always good to have her feeling better and for all of us to get home to our own beds.

* * *

Jenelle was at school for her last day of grade one to say goodbye to her classmates and teachers. We had a plan for the summer months that included Gail. Angus also told us that he would like to stop in for a visit over their vacation time.

Her respiratory problems persisted, she tired very easily and her colour was pale or cyanotic (blue). Her incredible smile would, yet again, lighten our concern and make us believers that we would get through this together. Some days she seemed to have more faith in her medical intervention than I did!

* * *

In late July we were back to emergency in Nanaimo. Jenelle's respirations were very shallow, her colour was poor, and she was listless. Her oxygen saturation was very low. Again a call was placed to the Cardiology Department at BC Children's Hospital. Immediately, a helicopter and medical team were on their way. Once again Mike was there to share our concern and offer hugs.

Within an hour of Jenelle's arrival in emergency she was in the operating room. The doctors drained seven cups of fluid from the pericardium, the sac around her heart. They left a drain in the sac and over the following twenty-four hours it drained another cup of fluid. An amazing accumulation from such a petite Angel.

* * *

Jenelle did well post-operatively and several days later was discharged from hospital. I told the doctors that I was concerned about bringing her home to Nanaimo as the echocardiogram and chest X-ray both indicated that the fluid was again starting to build up. They assured us that this was to be expected and to go to emergency in Nanaimo if I was anxious about her condition.

Ten days later my fears were to materialize. Jenelle was seen in emergency, the Cardiology department at BC Children's Hospital was called and the helicopter and medical team was on its way. With Mike there to wish us well and to offer the now familiar words of encouragement that he would see us soon back in Nanaimo, we were on our way. This time when we arrived there was a cardiac surgeon waiting for us. Dr. LaBlanc had arranged operating room time for Jenelle. He would create a window two centimetres in diameter in her pericardium, the sac around her heart. This time another two cups of fluid would be removed from the sac.

Dr. LaBlanc spoke with us following the surgery and said Jenelle tolerated the procedure well. When we were able to see Jenelle in Intensive Care she looked so peaceful and so much better. Her colour had improved and her respirations were easy, something we hadn't seen for way too long. She had two drains, one in her pericardium behind her heart and one in her chest. Both were draining serous fluid.

Ten days later we were once again on our way home. Jenelle would now be taking steroids for at least three months. She was also to be on a nebuliser twice a day to keep her breathing easy.

* * *

Gail came to our home for four hours most days to spend time with Jenelle. We were all so pleased that she showed complete memory recall to her communication program. Pleased but not surprised — this of course was our Angel that did everything just her way!

* * *

In September Jenelle started back to school. Wendi's class was now a grade one/two split so she was once again Jenelle's teacher and this was a good thing! Gail continued as her assistant and Angus was able to remain her "protector" in the same class.

She celebrated her eighth birthday feeling well and smiling at her party with her friends.

Our Christmas letter from 2002 reads

Jenelle had a horrendous year health wise but after heart surgery at BC Children's Hospital in August she has had an awesome autumn up until two weeks ago when she came down with a virus which has made life pretty miserable but hopefully she will be healthy again in time for Christmas.

Mo and I had decided that the time had come for him to retire from his second career and bring to an end his years in the picture framing business. We planned on selling our wonderful old home. It was time for a newer home which was more adaptable for Jenelle's needs. It was to be a busy but exciting year with lots of planning and dreams!

* * *

The New Year of 2003 began with an appointment at BC Children's Hospital for an assessment of Jenelle's overall health issues. Dr. Sandor, her cardiologist, reported that her cardiac condition was stable and that her tests "looked good for Jenelle."

Dr. Sear, her respirologist, told us that her lungs were very damaged and that her future would have more lung than heart complications.

Our long-time paediatrician, Jane Hailey, acknowledged our concern but she knew, as we did, that the experts should not rule out the invincible spirit of our Angel!

We had sold our home and purchased another. It had a level entry for Jenelle's wheelchair and not only a den for the three of us but her very own bedroom. We bought teddy bear wallpaper and had a theme of teddy bears for all her accessories. We were to take possession on August 1st. There was also a self-contained suite downstairs so that if the time came to have a Nanny to help with Jenelle's care we would be prepared. In the meantime, it would be great for family visits!

* * *

We knew that Jenelle's school, Princess Anne, was slated for closure in June of 2004. As our new home was in another part of the city we would have to drive her to school each day for the year if she remained with her friends at Princess Anne. We discussed it with many people and decided that perhaps the best action was to start afresh in September at the new school close to our new home. Jenelle, Gail and I went for a visit to Randerson Ridge School and we felt comfortable that Jenelle would be respected and accepted there.

* * *

The month of June was a stormy one for Jenelle's health issues but by the end of the month she was feeling much better and was able to return to school for the last days of her grade two year. It was difficult to explain to her classmates, particularly Angus, why she would not be returning in September. Angus was concerned that she would have no one there to protect her! On the last day of school she was given so many notes and drawings telling her how much she would be missed that Mo and I did wonder if we had made the right decision in deciding to transfer her to a new school!

* * *

The Canada Day long weekend was sunny and warm so we left early to spend a few days at the cabin. On the second day Jenelle was not feeling well. I couldn't put my finger on what was wrong; it was just not a good feeling for either of us. We came home so she could be as comfortable as possible in her own room. By that evening we were in Emergency.

I explained that there was something different happening. She was vomiting, which she seldom did, she was restless and squirming, again something she just did not do. I felt she was in pain although we knew from her past that she had a very high pain tolerance. The doctors thought that she had a flu and pneumonia. We returned home.

It was a very long night with none of us getting any sleep. Early in the morning I was holding Jenelle, she was so uncomfortable. As I gazed down at her there was a little tear drifting down her cheek. In all the years we had known and loved her, Jenelle had never before shed a tear. Now I knew there was something terribly wrong.

We returned to Emergency. The doctor ordered an X-ray of her abdomen. It was not good news. BC Children's Hospital was called and a helicopter was on its way once more. A good friend, Debbie, was working that day in the department and was a special blessing for us. As it was the July 1st holiday, I thought perhaps I would not call Mike until the next day. Debbie obviously realized how serious Jenelle's condition was and suggested that indeed I should call him. As always, he was there very quickly and stayed to watch Jenelle and me until we were in the air.

We were received in the emergency department with much concern. A surgeon was awaiting our arrival. It wasn't long after Mo appeared that Jenelle was taken to surgery.

It was a very difficult few hours waiting to hear what was wrong with our precious Angel.

With grave concern the surgeon told us that Jenelle was in critical condition. She had suffered a perforated bowel as a complication of a volvulus. The memory of the Italian doctor in California who had fallen in love with Jenelle quickly surfaced in my thinking. He had told us that Jenelle had all the classic symptoms of *CdLS* but for the bowel complication called a volvulus. Now she had completed her mission to be the perfect text book child!

I had many calls from Mike in the days following her surgery. He asked if I had seen the incredible double rainbow in the sky as we left Nanaimo. As he watched Jenelle and me and the extraordinary medical team leave in the helicopter for BC Children's Hospital he had witnessed a rainbow which seemed to encircle us. My eyes had not left Jenelle and I had not seen the sight that had so impressed him.

One of the songs we used to play often for Jenelle was "Somewhere over the Rainbow." We had brought her tape recorder to the hospital and would play her favourite music. "Somewhere over the Rainbow" became important for all of us.

> Somewhere over the rainbow,
> Way up high
> There's a land that I heard of
> Once in a lullaby.
>
> Somewhere over the rainbow,
> Skies are blue
> And the dreams that you dare to dream
> Really do come true.
>
> Some day I'll wish upon a star
> And wake up where the clouds are far behind me.
> Where troubles melt like lemon drops
> Away above the chimney tops
> That's where you'll find me.
>
> Somewhere over the rainbow,
> Blue birds fly

Birds fly over the rainbow
Why, then, oh, why can't I?

If happy little bluebirds fly
Beyond the rainbow
Why, oh, why can't I?

E.Y. Harburg/Harold Arlen

* * *

We spent the following four days at Jenelle's bedside in the Intensive Care Unit at BC Children's Hospital. She was surrounded by so much love from family and friends and staff.

Then on Saturday evening, July 5th, 2003, she decided, as only Jenelle could do, in her own way, that it was time to say goodbye. As we held her I remembered the music of Andrea Bocelli that we had heard in Paris with Greg, "Time to Say Goodbye."

* * *

It was incomprehensible that Jenelle would not be coming home with us. As happened for the few days after Greg was born, I was again in a dream. This surely was not reality. So many times we had been told she was indeed very ill. But always she had proven the medical "experts" wrong. She was our Jenelle and she was invincible.

We would soon acknowledge that this was our new reality, it was not my dream. Jenelle was so very tired. She had given us 3207 days of a love so powerful that she had moved mountains. She was the nearest thing to Heaven on our Earth. There are no words that could ever express the heartbreak and sadness we felt. This little Angel who had never spoken a word, had never independently taken a step, who communicated in her own special way only with those who would listen, was now on her journey to a different place. We knew she would be dancing and singing in an Angel choir. Perhaps it was the right time to accept that the Angels in Heaven had called for her much sooner than we had planned.

As we were on the ferry back to Nanaimo we recognized that plans had to be made for her service. The church across from her school was also the church her Grandmother attended. If Mike and Jenelle's family agreed, it seemed the right choice. My concern? It was a beautiful church, but it was large. I remember sharing with Mo my concern that not many people would come. I didn't like the thoughts of a large room with few people. Mo assured me it would be perfect. I didn't have the energy to disagree.

* * *

Once we arrived home it was difficult seeing all of Jenelle's treasures. When we had left for Vancouver, we never would have dreamed we would be returning without her. How were we going to survive?

* * *

We were amazed at how quickly her network of friends and family knew of her death. Friends were with us, flowers appeared, food arrived, phone calls expressing the pain and anguish that we felt were shared by so many.

I posted a message on the parents' support group of the International *CdLS* website.

Subject: "Heaven's Newest Angel"

Our hearts have been broken and it is especially difficult to tell you that our precious Jenelle has lost her struggle and is flying and singing with the Angels. She had an uphill mountain with a summit too high after a bowel volvulus that caused a horrendous infection. It is an unbelievable sadness for us but to know that she is in a better place helps ease the pain.

Soon messages were arriving from around the world. It was overwhelming the impact Jenelle had on so very many people. She had loved and she had been loved!

* * *

Her family, her social workers including and most importantly Mike, the Minister, Mo and I met in our living room to plan her service.

Jenelle's Mom and Grandma were sitting with their backs to the window. I was facing them. I was not paying attention to the conversation as I had noticed a hummingbird at the flower basket that

Jenelle loved to smell. Days before we had left for Vancouver, Mo and I had commented that there had not been any hummingbirds at the basket all summer. In a heartbeat the hummingbird was hovering at the window between her Mom and her Grandma. It seemed to be enjoying the conversation and the gathering of this group. I could not move. It surely was Jenelle's spirit checking us out! After everyone had left I mentioned it to Mo. He, too, had observed the spectacle and also noticed my reaction and knew exactly what I was feeling.

* * *

The following Saturday we arrived at the Church to a full parking lot. Mo had been right; the Church would not be empty. Her classmates, her therapists, her doctors, her friends, they were all there.

Gail, her wonderful school-time assistant, Elizabeth, who had cared for her so often when we were away and Art, my brother, who loved her unconditionally, gave the eulogies. Angus was there and he was assured that she would now be protected by the Angels but how thankful we were for all the years he had been her protector.

In the weeks following Jenelle's death I would call Elizabeth and Jan and sometimes Gail to come and help sort through her "stuff." Some days we would be able to get several drawers or boxes or cupboards organized. Some days we would have a few tears and a glass of wine and call it a day!

* * *

Jenelle's medical supplies, her glasses, her hearing aides were all given to another friend to be sent to *Doctors Without Borders* when the local group left later that year for Central America. I remembered that years earlier I had asked Greg if I could donate his old prostheses (his artificial arms) to a needy country. He had said "no," that they were his arms, and then asked, "would you want to give your arms away?!" Now, when I asked if his arms could accompany Jenelle's equipment he said "of course." It was quite the package that we were able to send to those who would have an improved life because of these two special people.

* * *

Our first time back to the cabin after Jenelle's passing was difficult. Again we would never have thought when we left that day in July that her life was so near fulfillment. Our cabin friends were all there. We were gathered in the sunshine for the last visit of the season. There seemed to be a sudden lull in conversation when someone remarked it was the first time they had ever seen a hummingbird at the cabins. I could not even glance where they were looking. Someone asked if I was feeling all right. Mo said I had suddenly gone very pale. When I told the story of the hummingbird at our basket when we were planning Jenelle's service there was a moment of reverence. It appeared we were all aware of her presence.

A few weeks later we were given a beautiful stained glass hummingbird from these same friends. It adorns a very special window in our home.

* * *

We did move into our new home but we didn't stay long. It just didn't seem right without Jenelle. We quickly sold the house and moved once again, this time into a small home in an area for those over fifty-five years! Each year our neighbours have two or three hummingbirds at their feeders. Each year we have a single hummingbird, both at the cabin and at our home, that spends long periods at our hanging baskets. We know why we believe!

Legends say that hummingbirds float free of time, carrying our hopes for love, joy and celebration. The hummingbird's delicate grace reminds us that life is rich, beauty is everywhere, every personal connection has meaning and that laughter is life's sweetest creation.

Author Unknown

I would often re-read the messages and the cards we had been sent after Jenelle's death. One card reads:

Remembrances

We can't feel saddened over the loss of those we love without first remembering the joy of loving them. The real sadness would have been never having had them in our lives at all. Remembering is a journey the heart takes, back into a time that was, and our thoughts are the only tickets needed to ride. We who have truly loved are blessed. Remember everything.

From Gerald, her link with the world of communication:

I am saddened to hear that Jenelle has passed away. She had a spark that drew people to her and that brought out a better side in people around her. I am happy however, that she had those years with Gail in Wendi's class, where she was in the midst of other kids, and interested in them, and interacting with them. When a life is so short it is somehow all the more important that the child be as actively and consciously in contact with her world as she can be; and I feel strongly that you, with the help you recruited from Princess Anne, the school district, the outreach program and elsewhere, brought Jenelle wonderfully into contact and interaction with her world and her age-mates. Your willing efforts and those of the friends you gathered around her combined with Jenelle's own zest for living to make a life about which there is much to celebrate. Thank you for bringing me into Jenelle's circle. It has been a joy to work with her and with you.

Sincerely

Gerald

* * *

I now look back on that time and really don't recall a lot. I guess my dream-like trance was a good way to cope. One day, watching the *Oprah* show she was discussing the death of a child and how you have a choice to dwell on their death or to celebrate their life. I realized it would not necessarily be an easy thing to do but the right thing to do.

And, so, this journal is my way to express the wonderful life, the wonderful being, the wonderful Angel that shared her life with us for those eight-plus years. Jenelle, I thank you from the bottom of my heart for allowing me to be the person selected to share so much of that life with you.

LIFE GOES ON

One of the many doctors we had met at the Conference in California in 2001 was Dr. Laird Jackson. He was a Professor of Genetics at the Drexel University College of Medicine in Philadelphia. The letter we received from him after Jenelle's death reads:

I am very sorry to hear of your loss. Dr. Kline has indicated that records are being sought. I have suggested to both Dr. Kline and Dr. Krantz that an investigation of the causes of death in CdL individuals is overdue. A project to gather information and attempt to document potentially preventable medical situations might avoid some of these agonizing episodes. I thank you for your willingness to help in this and will try to move this ahead and keep you informed of our progress.

* * *

In May of 2004 we received a letter from Dr. Krantz and his team at The Children's Hospital of Philadelphia that the *Cornelia de Lange Syndrome* gene had been identified. Jenelle had been a part of the research. "The *CdLS* gene has been found. One of the immediate advantages of identifying the gene is that we now have a means to directly test individuals with *CdLS* by means of a blood test to confirm diagnosis. We now know that if the words *CdLS* are introduced into the life of a family, their journey will be a little easier."

* * *

In July of 2005 our copy of *Reaching Out*, the newsletter from the *CdLS* Foundation arrived. There was an article entitled "Medical Alert Cards; Vital Information." Here was a card to be used for all those with *CdLS*. "The Medical Alert Card has been designed to provide information that is not only specific to your child but also outlines possible medical challenges specific to *CdLS*."

I have a copy of the email I sent to Dr. Jackson dated July 5th, 2005, and his response.

I felt I had to drop you a note to say how ironic life can be. It is two years to the day since Jenelle died and in this morning's mail was the latest copy of Reaching Out. The Medic Alert Card listing the life threatening conditions and the first being GI problems and Volvulus was amazing! We really do believe she was with us and left us to make the world a better place for CdLS *kids. Some family will have this card with them, some medical professional will see it and perhaps a life can be saved. We are well, doing respite care for two very involved special needs kids and spending lots of time with our grandchildren.*

He replied

It is nice to hear from you and to hear of your satisfying work. I too am happy that the alert card got done. We have more work to do to inform the medical community about the kids and what to watch for. I am still at work on an updated database to gather this information and focus attention on the practical problems. I will be back in contact with you as this work goes on.

All of this only confirmed what we had acknowledged all along, the fact that Jenelle had been sent to our earth to teach all of us. She was a part of research.

* * *

And, yes, as you may recall, I encouraged Trudy, Michael's Mom, not to get involved with caring for these special little people. Nonetheless, Mo and I have continued to accept these challenges. When we began to discuss the idea, Glen was hesitant that I would get too involved and be heartbroken again. I could honestly assure him it would only be as a respite home. We knew too well what a difference it could make in a family's life to have an occasional rest from the physical and emotional demands and the responsibility of loving and caring for these children every day and every night.

* * *

And, so, in our lives, we currently have two adorable young people who come for a sleep over on occasion. Hailey is seven years old and diagnosed with cerebral palsy. She is in a wheelchair, is tube fed, non-verbal and is the most beautiful red haired, blue-eyed little girl you would ever hope to meet. She has wonderful parents and a very busy, very handsome young brother who is nearly four.

Ryan has a chromosomal abnormality and is six years old. He is also tube fed and non-verbal, but is in Kindergarten and has Gerald in his life for communication as he is hearing and vision impaired as Jenelle was. He has made amazing progress and it is a pleasure to observe his delight as he is able to convey his thoughts and be understood. He has an extraordinary Mom; they are so in love with one another. We feel very privileged to be a part of their lives.

Our friend Debbie, who was in the Emergency Department in Nanaimo when Jenelle and I left on our last helicopter ride, has also remained a constant in our lives. She too has a "special" daughter; Kelly is nearing eighteen and has *Cohen Syndrome*. It too is a chromosomal abnormality with a host of symptoms. Kelly is a real challenge for her Mom who continues to work in the Emergency Department at the local hospital. The two of them make a dynamic duo and with a team of associates to help in Kelly's care, they enjoy, as best the can, their life in Holland!

* * *

We often go to our cemetery to visit with Jenelle. We planted a honey locust tree in her memory. On the plaque at the base of her tree is the inscription:

~~~ Jenelle ~~~

Sept. 24 1994 till July 5 2003

Some people only see Angels,
We held one in our arms.

Jenelle, you will be loved and remembered forever…We send hugs to Heaven each time we see a hummingbird or a rainbow…We miss you…our little Angel.

We keep fresh flowers in her vase when the weather permits; she loved her flowers so!

* * *

"I know for sure that every person in the world has a purpose for being here — a calling. The work of your life is to discover that purpose and get on with the business of living it out. The only courage you need is the courage to find and follow your passion."

Oprah Winfrey

I am so fortunate — I discovered my purpose — I found the courage — I followed my passion. I went to Holland and had a wonderful stay.

Hazel

CONCLUSION

"Celebrating Holland — I'm home"

I have been in Holland for over a decade now. It has become home. I have had time to catch my breath, to settle and adjust, to accept something different than I'd planned.

I reflect back on those years of past when I had first landed in Holland. I remember clearly my shock, my fear, my anger — the pain and uncertainty. In those first few years, I tried to get back to Italy as planned, but Holland was where I was to stay. Today, I can say how far I have come on this unexpected journey. I have learned so much more. But, this too has been a journey of time.

I worked hard. I bought new guidebooks. I learned a new language and I slowly found my way around this new land. I have met others whose plans had changed like mine, and who could share my experience. We supported one another and some have become very special friends.

Some of these fellow travellers had been in Holland longer than I and were seasoned guides, assisting me along the way. Many have encouraged me. Many have taught me to open my eyes to the wonder and gifts to behold in this new land. I have discovered a community of caring. Holland wasn't so bad.

I think that Holland is used to wayward travellers like me and grew to become a land of hospitality, reaching out to welcome, to assist and to support newcomers like me in this new land. Over the years, I've wondered what life would have been like if I'd landed in Italy as planned. Would life have been easier? Would it have been as rewarding? Would I have learned some of the important lessons I hold today?

Sure, this journey has been more challenging and at times I would (and still do) stamp my feet and cry out in frustration and protest.

And, yes, Holland is slower paced than Italy and less flashy than Italy, but this too has been an unexpected gift. I have learned to slow down in ways too and look closer at things, with a new appreciation for the remarkable beauty of Holland with its tulips, windmills and Rembrandts.

I have learned to love Holland and call it Home.

I have become a world traveller and discovered that it doesn't matter where you land. What's more important is what you make of your journey and how you see and enjoy the very special, the very lovely, things that Holland, or any land, has to offer.

Yes, over a decade ago I landed in a place I hadn't planned. Yet I am thankful, for this destination has been richer than I could have imagined!"

Cathy Anthony